Peter Woolley

Drawing towards Watercolour

Exercises and techniques for improving your paintings

David and Charles

Endpaper:
SUMMER IN GRASSINGTON
38 x 56cm (15 x 22in)

Title page:
SUNRISE OVER OTLEY
17 x 56cm (10 x 22in)

Above:
SUNRISE OVER THE GREAT RIDGE
17 x 56cm (10 x 22in)

A DAVID & CHARLES BOOK
David & Charles is a subsidiary of F+W (UK) Ltd.,
an F+W Publications Inc. company

First published in the UK in 2005

Copyright © Peter Woolley 2005

Distributed in North America
by F+W Publications, Inc.
4700 East Galbraith Road
Cincinnati, OH 45236
1-800-289-0963

Peter Woolley has asserted his right to be identified as author of this work
in accordance with the Copyright, Designs and Patents Act, 1988.

A catalogue record for this book is available from the British Library.

ISBN 0 7153 1994 9 hardback
ISBN 0 7153 1998 1 paperback (USA only)

Printed in Singapore by KHL Printing Co. Pte Ltd
for David & Charles
Brunel House   Newton Abbot   Devon

Commissioning Editor Mic Cady
Desk Editor Lewis Birchon
Art Editor Sue Cleave
Project Editor Ian Kearey
Production Controller Kelly Smith

Visit our website at www.davidandcharles.co.uk

David & Charles books are available from all good bookshops; alternatively
you can contact our Orderline on (0)1626 334555 or write to us at
FREEPOST EX2 110, David & Charles Direct, Newton Abbot, TQ12 4ZZ
(no stamp required UK mainland).

THE AUTHOR

Peter Woolley has been a professional watercolour
artist since 1986. His original work can be found in
private collections all over the world, and many of his
paintings are available as limited edition prints and
cards. He tours extensively and runs regular tuition
courses. View more of Peter's work at
www.peterwoolley.co.uk

CONTENTS

INTRODUCTION

THE LAST GLIMMER, BARE HOUSE
17 x 26cm (7x 10in)

Below:
AUTUMN ON BUTHERLYP HOWE
28 x 38cm (11x 15in)

Many people who start painting in watercolour begin by working directly from photographs, either from books or magazines, or from ones they have taken themselves. This is fine, since it is here that the humble beginnings of taking a greater visual interest in our surroundings often take a hold. A link must, at some point, be made between how we see things with our eyes and how we translate what we see into paint, and photographs are a great vehicle through which to do this, offering us the opportunity to observe the landscape at leisure. A real-life landscape that we can stand in, walk through, view in 360 degrees and whose air we can breathe, is a three-dimensional experience. A photograph takes us part-way along the road to flattening that three-dimensional, scene into a two-dimensional one – a process we must inevitably go through if we are to paint it in watercolour.

The novice painter soon realizes how much has been taken for granted, and that there is so much more to the surroundings than first meets the eye. At this point, our desire to capture a subject in paint is tempered only by a growing awareness that we've never really looked so closely at it before now. The idea of working purely from sketches tends to scare many people off. What about colour? If I'm drawing only in pencil, how will I remember the colours? What if my drawing abilities are not up to the job? If my initial sketch is not up to scratch, won't my final painting also be substandard?

These fears are entirely understandable. Watercolour is an unforgiving medium and starting out can be a daunting experience, either with a group or teaching yourself at home, and you could be forgiven for thinking that working from sketches is going to multiply your already mounting problems when it comes to making any sort of progress.

What follows can be seen either as a strict, graded, work-through course or a pleasant meander through the world of watercolour according to me, where the examples and exercises are for you to dip into and explore at your own pace. If you are new to watercolour, I recommend you take the time to work through each chapter carefully before moving on to the next. If you already have watercolour experience, but are looking to work more with sketches, headings are used to make identification between the two disciplines easier.

The chapters in this book are grouped into subjects, and the content of each one graded from simple introductory exercises through to a fully fledged step-by-step project chosen to illustrate that particular subject. Throughout, I've tried to maintain a link between what can be achieved in pencil-sketch form and its watercolour counterpart. Success is proportional to practice, so I recommend you tackle the exercises one at a time. If your first attempt is unsuccessful, repeat it. If your first attempt is a riotous success, then repeat it again anyway, just to be sure it wasn't a fluke!

The projects featured at the end of each chapter vary quite considerably in complexity and should be tackled at a pace you're most comfortable with. Don't worry if yours doesn't look quite the same; the most important thing is to have a go! Feel free to reproduce the subjects as close to the original style as you can; ultimately, of course, I would hope that the work here is sufficiently inspiring for you to hunt down similar subjects entirely of your own making, where all the thought processes, compositional decision-making and planning can be 100 per cent attributable to you.

WORKING IN WATERCOLOUR

There is no doubt about it: watercolour is a frustrating medium to master. At times it seems as if it has a mind of its own, and progress can often seem like two steps forward followed by one step back. Unfortunately there are no short-cuts – if you want to succeed, the secret is perseverance. I often say to students that before learning about how to apply the paint, they should take a look deep within themselves and start developing a thick skin with which to deal with those moments of acute disappointment.

Bask in those moments of glory when everything seems to go right (and it will). Remember, it's perfectly natural to be hypercritical of your own work – we all do it: if there's a weakness in our painting, it'll jump out and upset us every time we look at it, but that doesn't mean that others will spot it. Take comfort in the knowledge that it happens to everyone at some point.

Naturally, different people learn and progress at different rates, so avoid comparing yourself too closely to others around you (this applies particularly to those who learn in groups or classes).

Finally, as you do improve, continue to take stock of what you have achieved. Always save your work, however bad you think it is, so that you can look back over where you've been. And as you do improve, push the boundaries. Very often, students reach a stage at which they feel very comfortable and find that they get into a bit of a rut; suddenly the way forward seems unclear, and all their achievements seem to be behind them. So every now and then, live a little dangerously: break out of what might be called the Comfort Zone. You have nothing to lose, and potentially everything to gain. Remember, no one person knows it all – however much experience you gain painting at the easel, there is always something more to learn!

MATERIALS

Sketching

 Sketching requires so little in the way of materials, I'm certain it's one of the reasons I'm drawn (pardon the pun) towards it so much. Most forms of art tend to require great amounts of gear most of the time, and the constant need to replenish and increase equipment means that something requiring so little to complete the task as sketching can be looked upon as a breath of fresh air.

All you need for sketching is a pencil (I recommend a 2B grade: anything softer requires constant sharpening, and anything harder will fail to produce the range of tone required), a sketchbook, an eraser and something to sharpen your pencil with (I prefer to use a craft blade since pencil sharpeners can tend to devour your tools at an alarming rate, especially those awful electronic ones).

Sketchpads come in all makes and sizes. While A5 is a convenient size for portability, A4 or A3 are ideal for larger subjects. Sketchpads that come with a slightly textured surface are good for sketching.

Watercolour

 Buying art materials for the first time can be a daunting experience, not to say an expensive one. What follows are the basic requirements needed to paint in watercolour: I've attempted to keep the list to a minimum, offering cost-cutting alternatives wherever possible. Some items can often be picked up quite cheaply, while others shouldn't be bought from anywhere but a reputable art supplier.

PAINT

Watercolour paint comes in either tubes or pots called pans or half-pans. Although choosing between the two is largely a matter of personal choice, it is generally accepted that a far richer mix of colours can be achieved, and with greater speed and efficiency, by squeezing paint fresh from a tube.

Paint also comes in two qualities: artists' or students'. Artists'-quality paints are more expensive because they are manufactured using the best, most pure ingredients, providing greater lightfastness, durability and mixing ability. Since cost can be a major factor when starting out, many beginners, quite understandably, purchase students' colours. These are OK for getting started, but I would strongly recommend replenishing your stock, as you use it up, with artists'-quality – you'll never go back!

There are many manufacturers of watercolour paints to choose from, the largest and most widely available being Winsor & Newton and Daler Rowney. Maimeri are also highly regarded, as are those produced by the SAA (Society for All Artists), but there are many other brands, each with its own enthusiasts. The watercolours in this book were painted using Winsor & Newton and SAA paints.

COLOURS

An artist's choice of colours (otherwise known as his or her palette) is a very personal thing, and one that can distinguish one person's work from another – for instance, yellow ochre is a colour that I've never got on well with, yet there are many artists who wouldn't be seen dead without it. I encourage students to work with as few colours as possible to promote a more simple, harmonious finish to their work.

Below are the colours in my palette, with which all the demonstration subjects in this book have been produced. They've worked well for me over the years, but are by no means a definitive set. If you're completely new to painting, I recommend experimenting with a variety of colours to discover which ones you like most of all, then trimming the list down to a similar list of about eight colours.

| Payne's grey | French ultramarine | Winsor blue (red shade) | Burnt umber | Raw sienna | Cadmium yellow | Cadmium red | Alizarin crimson |

I don't use commercially manufactured greens, which tend to stain and can be difficult to work with. Like many other artists, I prefer to mix my own, which, with a little experimentation, are often more natural in appearance (see page 11 for more information about mixing greens).

BRUSHES

It isn't necessary to buy the most expensive brushes you can find, unless your budget can run to it, but it's also not a good idea to go for the cheapest: for example, nylon brushes don't hold the water as well and lose their point quickly. Brushes made of a synthetic/sable mix from a reputable manufacturer are probably your best choice.

A stencil brush is an excellent tool to keep in your kit as a last resort for removing areas of a painting that have gone horribly wrong, for reclaiming highlights or just lightening an area of wash. With careful scrubbing using clean water, the brush should be able to remove pigment without damaging the surface of the paper too much (if you remove too much surface from your paper, you may damage the size coat, and the result will be like painting on blotting paper).

PAPER

Whatever your ability, watercolour paper is one area in which you simply cannot afford to make too many cutbacks. First and foremost, you must use watercolour paper and not cartridge (sketchbook) paper. It can be bought in books or sheets, and comes in 180gsm (90lb), 300gsm (140lb), 410gsm (200lb) and 600gsm (300lb) weights, with a choice of four different surfaces: Hot-Pressed or HP (smooth surface), NOT, Cold-Pressed or CP (slightly textured) or Rough (which rather speaks for itself). As a landscape painter, I always use Rough paper, as many textural effects can only be created on this paper. There are many brands to choose from, but my personal favourites are Arches 600gsm (300lb) or Saunders Waterford 410gsm (200lb).

STRETCHING PAPER

Paper lighter than 410gsm (200lb) is prone to extreme 'cockling' (wrinkling and buckling) when large amounts of water are used, and it is therefore advisable to stretch it before use.

1 Thoroughly soak the paper in water for a few minutes. The water can be warm, but not hot, as this can damage the size coat; or you can play safe and use cold water. Knock off the drips and position the damp paper on the painting board. Dab the edges dry (where the tape is going to go) with a towel.

2 Tape the paper down with gummed brown paper tape. It's a good idea to tear your tape to size before getting your hands wet.

3 Work out any air pockets with the towel and leave the paper to dry flat – do not be tempted to prop it up by a radiator, as all the moisture will run to the bottom edge and the tape there will become unstuck. Once the paper is dry, you will have a perfectly drum-like flat surface upon which to work, that is less susceptible to cockling.

OTHER MATERIALS

PALETTES

Mixing palettes come in all shapes and sizes, from extremely simple to very complex-looking, and from plastic to ceramic. If you're doing it on the cheap, two or three old saucers should be more than sufficient. What is most important is that you have a clearly defined area for squeezing your paint out (if you're working from tubes, that is) and somewhere to do the actual mixing. It doesn't matter if your mixing area is plastic or ceramic, so long as it is white (or light-coloured); trying to mix paint on a dark surface is not doing yourself any favours.

WATER CONTAINERS

Water for mixing can be stored in anything you have to hand. Old glass jars are probably best, while empty yogurt pots offer the added convenience that you can stack them neatly after use. An artist friend of mine even uses a huge metal dog bowl.

BOARDS

You will need a board to which to attach your paper. This needs to be quite rigid to prevent it from bending during the paper-stretching process: 6mm (¼in) MDF or plywood is ideal for the job.

EASELS

Whether or not to invest in an easel is a personal choice. I've always preferred metal ones to wood, as they don't seem to wear out so quickly (and I've always found erecting a wooden easel to be on a par with putting up a deckchair). Using an easel isn't mandatory, but if you're going to work on a table, you'll need something to prop your board up to achieve any sort of success with those big washes; many table easels are available at reasonable prices, or you could head for the workshop armed with hammer and nails and fashion something of your own design.

RUCKSACK

For outdoor work, a small, lightweight backpack or rucksack is a wise investment, enabling you to also carry a small paintbox and watercolour pad, waterproof clothing and provisions. The one I use has a convenient stand that folds out and converts the whole thing into a useful seat.

Mixing paint

Mixing paint is one of those great perceived mysteries of watercolour, the process of which I am most frequently quizzed about by students of all abilities: 'I just can't seem to mix my paints properly', or 'I have a go, but I'm not really sure what it is I'm doing or what I'm supposed to be doing' are common statements.

I say 'mystery', though there really is no mystery to it. If you've never done it before, it's natural to get a little anxious about mixing colours. The key to success is perseverance.

There is no better way of learning and improving your understanding of the mixing process than practice. Everyone is different. When you load a brush with paint, this is an activity peculiar to you, and while 'One part this and two parts that' may go some way towards easing the learning curve, you should observe very closely what happens every time you mix paint.

Experiment with paint. Don't be embarrassed: apply it to paper in different consistencies (from weak and watery to thick and gooey) with a wide range of brushes, and see how it looks on the paper. Experiment by deliberately adding wet paint to wet paint and watch how the brushstrokes interact and bleed into one another.

If you're completely new to watercolour and unsure about how to produce a basic, single-colour mix in your palette, work through the method described. With perseverance, in time you will become as one with your brush, and mixing paint will no longer be a mystery.

TONAL RANGE
This is how French ultramarine looks after repeatedly adding water to the mix. The difference between its darkest and lightest values is referred to as its tonal range.

MIXING COLOURS

1 Prepare a pot or jar of clean water. Your mixing palette should be divided into two definite areas: one to store paint in, either from a tube or a pan, and a second area in which to do the actual mixing. Paint should always be transferred a bit at a time from the storage area to the mixing area using the brush, as this way, you retain maximum control over the mix.

Load a large, flat wash brush or a large round brush (Nos 12–16) with clean water by dipping it into your water jar. Transfer the water to the mixing area of your palette by dragging the bristles against the side to unload it.

2 Dip the tip of the brush into the squeezed paint to reload it. If you are using paint freshly squeezed from the tube, don't overload it. If you are working from pans, work the damp bristles of the brush into the pigment to soften it up first.

3 Transfer the paint into the waiting water and mash it about a bit. The paint and water must be well mixed before it is applied to the paper. If it isn't, neat, undiluted pigment, which can be difficult to remove, may mark the paper and play havoc with your nice smooth wash.

Repeat steps 2 and 3 until your mix is of the desired intensity. Adding more paint will darken it and make a 'richer' mix, while adding more water will weaken and lighten the mix. Until you're confident at being able to accurately assess your mix by sight alone, always test it on a spare piece of watercolour paper. If it's too dark, add more water; if it's too weak and light, add more paint.

Practise mixing colours together, both in the pot and on the paper. The mix shown above is used frequently throughout this book: adding burnt umber to French ultramarine in very small quantities at a time has the effect of 'neutralizing' it and creating a useful blue/grey mix, ideal for stone and other natural effects.

TESTING COLOURS

It's a good idea always to have a sheet of scrap paper, of the same type that you intend to paint on, handy when mixing. The colour may look OK in the pot, but how does it look on the paper? Quite simply, the more you do it, the more familiar you will become with what you can achieve.

Adding a tiny amount of alizarin crimson to the same mix above left has the effect of warming it up slightly.

When mixing green, I begin with cadmium yellow and Winsor blue (red shade). Both err on the warm (red) side, and create a clean, fresh green (above). For a more natural, olive-looking green, add tiny amounts of burnt umber to the mix until you get the colour you're looking for. A similar, but less bright set of colours can be obtained by switching Winsor blue with French ultramarine, the granulating properties of which can provide a welcome hint of texture.

MIXING GREENS

Green is a notoriously difficult colour to work with, and the notion that 'yellow and blue make green' can be slightly misleading. Believe it or not, green can be produced from some of the most unlikely and surprising combinations (lamp black and lemon yellow being one such example). The fact is, some combinations of yellow and blue only result in something resembling sludge, which can come as a bit of a shock to new painters, and one can hardly blame them for scouring the shelves for a commercially mixed and readily available alternative. But you can do better.

You may find that a mix that looks vibrant and fresh when first applied to paper, becomes drab and decidedly unvibrant when it has dried off. This is normal, and can be easily rectified by applying a further, weak wash (sometimes referred to as a 'glaze' in these circumstances) of cadmium yellow, which will have the effect of revitalizing the colour.

Starting out – basic exercises

After wax crayons, the humble pencil is probably the first art tool most of us encounter. Schoolchildren are introduced to pencils long before being entrusted to anything containing ink, presumably on the basis that the marks they make can be removed easily.

Where to begin, then? Well, the one thing, in my experience at least, that many beginners time and time again berate themselves for, is their inability to draw 'even a straight line' – so that seems as good a place as any to start.

STRAIGHT LINES

If you've never sketched before or you feel your drawing skills leave much to be desired, this is a good time to run through a few simple exercises to familiarize yourself with what methods are available.

Begin by practising some straight lines. The ability to draw a straight line without the aid of a ruler is something that comes with practice. Draw several straight lines parallel to your first, above and below. Vary the distances apart, and don't worry if they're a bit rough – this becomes a little easier the more you do.

Try drawing with a loose, free wrist-action, and keep telling yourself that furry lines are OK! Experiment a little, deliberately alternating between oversketched furry lines and then fine, precise lines.

Once you're happy (or bored) with your horizontal lines, try adding several vertical straight lines at 90 degrees to your existing ones – don't rotate the paper, as the object is to practise drawing horizontal and vertical lines from the same position. Remember: this is freehand drawing, so near enough is good enough!

Practise drawing straight lines without a ruler.

Add further lines, parallel to the first ones, then strengthen one of the inner boxes you've created by drawing over it. Finally, try shading in as neatly as you can.

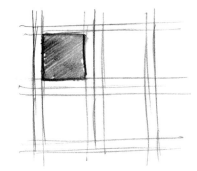

Now take your straight lines a step further, by attempting this simple exercise. Begin by sketching out the grid as shown here.

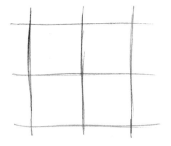

With a little imagination, your sketch can be developed into a window. Be as loose as possible with your pencil, and don't worry if it doesn't turn out exactly as this one.

PENCIL SHADING

Tone refers to the lightness or darkness of an object, quite irrespective of its colour. Although drawing is for the most part concerned with lines, some form of shading will inevitably become necessary to differentiate between the different tones inherent in a subject, and to help create the illusion of solidity and depth. There are two main forms of shading: a plain pattern, where the objective is to create a flat, even-looking surface, and a gradual pattern, where, as the name implies, there appears to be a graduation from a light tone to a dark tone.

PLAIN SHADING

To develop a successful shading technique, you should understand the basic drawing pattern you need to employ. Try drawing this pattern, which is the basis of plain shading.

Let your pencil travel across the paper, moving the wrist loosely up and down.

Now draw it again, but this time speed it up.

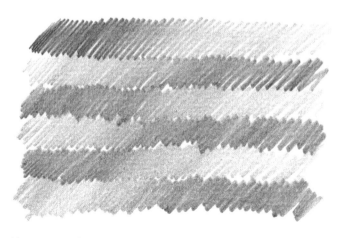

Repeat the process, but this time, as well as speeding up your drawing, tighten up the pattern. When you practise this simple piece of shading, don't worry too much about how neat it is, but try to get the pencil lines as tonally even as possible.

GRADUAL SHADING

Gradual shading is produced in the same way as plain shading, but a gradual increase or decrease of pressure on the pencil produces a lightening or darkening of the shaded area.

In many ways, shading can be seen as the pencil equivalent of the washes used in watercolour, and if the aim of this book is to encourage the development of paintings from the humble pencil sketch, this can be regarded as the first important link between the two disciplines and a good time to introduce you to the four basic washes, the building blocks from which all watercolour paintings are created.

Have a go at the example shown here, working slowly down the page and alternating the effect as you go. Always work in the same direction: left to right, or right to left if you are left-handed. Don't despair if the effect comes out rough to start with. You'll find it gets much easier as you proceed, because you'll slip into a rhythm of sorts.

Improving accuracy

One effective method of improving accuracy in your drawing is by attempting simple geometric shapes.

TRIANGLES

Begin by drawing yourself a triangle. Whilst concentrating on keeping your lines straight, you may discover that your third line doesn't meet up with the first line. Don't despair – practice makes perfect!

It is essential to try and achieve an optimum balance between speed and accuracy – draw quickly in freehand, but attempt to get the lines as parallel with each other as you can. Repeat the exercise several times using different shapes.

1 Repeat the process over and over again. Don't worry about the sides and corners of your triangles being of equal size – this isn't a mathematics exam.

2 Eventually your triangles will stop looking like strange three-sided beings from the planet Vague Triangle and start to look like something that might hold a large road bridge together.

3 Once you've gained confidence, practise drawing further, increasingly large triangles around the outer edge of your original shape. The challenge is to try and keep your lines as parallel as possible.

NEGATIVE DRAWING

One property shared between both drawing in pencil and watercolour is the fact that light tones cannot be created directly, only indirectly. In other words, a light object only appears light if you place a dark tone alongside it. If the light object is relatively simple in shape, it's unlikely to pose much of a problem. Something more complex, however, is going to take a little more practice. This method of shading around an object is known as negative drawing. Further examples of negative drawing can be seen on page 82.

In this relatively simple example, the church has been 'drawn around' in a negative fashion, as have the headstones in the adjoining churchyard.

This is more elaborate. Each branch of the sunlit tree has had to be drawn around in order to make highlight it against the dark background.

CIRCLES AND ELLIPSES

Now move on to different shapes. Prove to yourself that while triangles might be your forte, there are other shapes out there: squares, circles and more complex designs, such as five- or six-pointed stars or even completely original, non-categorizable shapes of your own making.

Circles can be troublesome at first. Without a convenient paint-tin lid to draw around, you'd be forgiven for thinking thoughts of despair. With practice, however, you'll soon discover that circles are no more difficult than any other shape. Practise drawing them freehand whenever you can – for example, if you're a doodler, use the time spent waiting on the end of a telephone for some serious circle practice.

1 It's a good idea to first get your hand moving in a circular motion above the paper, pencil poised, before making a mark.

2 Keep your lines light at first, and don't worry about their being furry. Once you're happy with the general shape you can go back over the lines, redrawing and sharpening them up.

Once you've gained enough confidence to draw the concentric circles design shown here, try shading in the circles. Beginning with a plain shading pattern, shade in alternate circles only (think target practice) then repeat the exercise, this time using an alternating graded shading pattern. To avoid it looking too untidy, keep your shading lines as near to the same angle as possible.

Finally, experiment with an irregular series of ellipses similar to the example shown. The most important thing is to ensure that your gradual shading patterns alternate smoothly, and always remember that the importance of tone – dark against light, and light against dark – is the priority.

ADDING DEPTH

Only a relatively small step is required to turn simple, two-dimensional shapes into three-dimensional-looking objects. This is the ultimate challenge for all artists tackling real subjects: to take three-dimensional objects that exist in a real, three-dimensional space and reproduce them convincingly on a two-dimensional surface.

What it all boils down to is the illusion of depth and space. While watercolour provides several means with which to achieve this visual trick, in pencil, all you have to do is think carefully about where the light is coming from and how it impacts upon the object.

Observation is the key. This may sound an obvious thing to say, but whatever the subject, be it landscape, still life or portrait, unless you take the time to really look at it, how are you ever really going to understand it? Representative art is 50 per cent observation, 30 per cent contemplation and 20 per cent graffiti. (Don't quote me on the percentages, though.)

To hone your drawing skills, it's a good idea to have a go at drawing anything and everything. Objects from the kitchen drawer are a good starting point, as are plants and furniture. Hand tools such as screwdrivers and spanners also make good still-life subjects.

1 To draw a convincing sphere, the area of shading should remain curved throughout, leaving a circular highlight. Begin by making a light, plain shading.

2 Gradually apply further shadings, with ever-increasing darker tones. With practice, you should be able to blend in and create an almost seamless curve. The graduated, ellipse-shaped shadow provides a touch of added realism.

Watercolour

PLAIN WASH

As its name implies, this wash is a flat, even layer of paint. It would be unusual to begin a painting with an all-over plain wash – it is more likely that you would apply it in later stages to smaller areas where an even colour is required. However plain, flat, uninteresting or just boring it may appear at first glance, a plain wash is the first step towards mastering the rudiments of watercolour.

Attach a small piece of 300gsm (140lb) paper to your painting board (which should be set at an angle of 20–30 degrees) with masking tape. If you don't have an easel, prop your board up with any object. Next, mix a large pot of medium-strength Winsor blue (Prussian blue is a good alternative). A vital point to remember is that all colours dry lighter than they appear when you first apply them.

If this is your first attempt at a plain wash, it may all seem a little too hard and complicated. Fear not! Practice most definitely makes perfect – the more washes you paint, the better at painting them you will become. Describing the process in detail (right) is one thing, but perfecting the result is quite another kettle of fish. It may be that your first attempt came out perfect. If so, do it again so as to prove to yourself that it was more than just luck! If your wash came out stripy, you may be overlapping brushmarks too much or applying too much pressure, thus removing what you have already applied, or you may just need to invest in a larger brush.

Painting off the end of the paper and on to the tape creates a clean edge to the wash when the tape is removed. Be aware, however, that any excess paint sitting on the tape is not going to dry and soak in the same time as it does on

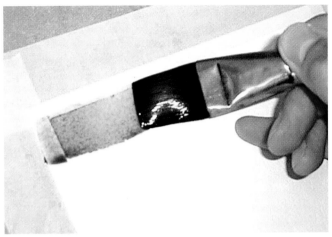

1 When you are happy with your mix (it wants to be neither too strong nor too weak), apply the paint to the dry surface of the paper in a slow, sweeping movement, keeping the brush at a steady speed, pressure and angle. If you are right-handed, then you should start in the top left-hand corner and paint from left to right (vice versa if you are left-handed). The paint will accumulate in a well along the bottom edge of the brushstroke – this is called 'beading', and is perfectly normal.

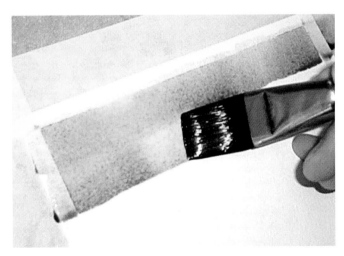

2 When you reach the opposite side, continue the brushstroke off the edge of the paper and on to the tape, then repeat the process by applying a second brushstroke below your first. This time, however, make sure your brush touches the previous stroke just enough to encourage the beading to flood into the new brushstroke. Because the board is set at a gentle angle, the paint will flow downwards and even out to create a smooth, seamless joint. Repeat the process until you have reached the bottom edge of the paper.

At some point, you will need to reload your brush. When your brush does run out of paint, the speckled, broken brushmark it creates is known as drybrush, and although useful, this technique is not welcome just now. Any uneven brushstrokes must be carefully painted over with a fresh mix.

the watercolour paper, so it's worth carefully dabbing the tape dry with a piece of tissue to avoid it seeping back on to a partially dried area of wash and creating an unseemly pattern known as a backrun (see right).

DRYBRUSH

As its name suggests, drybrush is created by removing most of the paint from your brush before applying it. This can happen accidentally, but it can easily be produced by dragging a loaded brush across a spare piece of paper until you have to apply extra pressure to make any sort of mark.

This technique works only on Rough paper, and is ideal for creating textures and effects, such as a sunburst on the surface of a lake.

USING DRYBRUSH In this simple watercolour, the sparkling sunburst effect on the surface of the lake was created using drybrush. Quite often, the drybrush effect can happen accidentally in the course of a painting: think positively about such occurrences and incorporate them into your work at every opportunity, as they can bring unexpected lightness and freshness to a composition.

BACKRUNS

Sometimes referred to as 'bleed-back', backruns are the scourge of all well-meaning watercolourists. If you bring water to a wash whose surface seems dry, but is still wet underneath, then it will soak through, joining forces with that unseen well of moisture, and the residual pigment will be carried along and deposited in a random fashion, to create a cauliflower-like pattern.

There isn't much you can do about backruns when they occur, except lift the whole area out and repaint it. The best way to look upon a backrun is to be cool about it – unless it's happened in a completely awkward place, try to make it a part of the composition and work it into the design of the painting (think of it as a happy accident); but remember: you can never get a decent backrun when you want one!

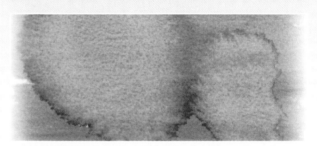

GRADED WASH

Where the plain wash concentrates on evenness and regularity, the graded or graduated wash gradually changes tone or colour. In other words, it can be a wash, painted in a single colour, that appears to change from a dark tone to a light tone over the length of its span, or it can be a wash that appears to change from one colour to another, say from blue to red, over the length of its span.

Both of the commonly used methods of creating a graded wash require the painting board, as with the plain wash, to be inclined at an angle of 20–30 degrees. Even if you prefer to paint on to a flat, horizontal surface, it is worth remembering that there are few certainties in watercolour. If you paint at a slight angle, you know which way the paint is going to flow. if nothing else. Gravity is an important ally in watercolour, so use it to your advantage wherever possible.

METHOD 1 The simplest, but not always the most successful, method of creating a graded wash is to produce it in exactly the same way as a plain wash, but as you work your way down the paper, keep adding small amounts of water to the mix to weaken, and therefore lighten it. The result is a wash consisting of a single colour, which appears dark and rich at the top, light, and weak and barely visible (if not invisible) at the bottom.

METHOD 2 A more effective way to produce a graded wash is to begin by thoroughly wetting the surface of the paper with an all-over wash of clean water. While the paper is still wet, apply your paint in steady brushstrokes, as before. Because you are now painting on to a wet surface, the mix should dilute and lighten in appearance all by itself. In fact, depending on the size of paper you're working on, it should be possible to produce the wash from a single loaded brush (it's worth making the mix slightly richer, with more paint than water in the mix, to compensate for the wet surface).

TIMING

Timing is, of course, crucial throughout watercolour, but never more so than in the creation of big washes. One of the most frequently asked questions at exhibitions (other than 'How long does it take to do a painting?' and 'Is that your best price?'), is 'How do you get your washes so smooth?'

The answer is, simply, timing. You must [a] ensure that your initial wetting of the paper is thorough, and [b] work quickly. If you don't take [a] or [b] sufficiently seriously, you're heading for disaster.

To maximize your painting time, it's a good idea to mix up your paint first. When I'm preparing to lay down a big wash, I wet the paper first, mix my colours, then wet the paper a second time before applying paint. Depending on your painting environment, the paper starts to absorb the clean water immediately, and paint mixed in a pot starts to dry out and evaporate as quickly, so you should constantly monitor the status of both the paper and the paint mix as you go along.

In this example, the sky was painted first, as a wet-in-wet wash, with the hill detail added after it had dried (leaving the trees and house as untouched highlights to be added later). The full painting can be seen on page 116.

MULTICOLOUR GRADED WASH

Up to now, we've been dealing with washes consisting of only one colour. A graded wash can also be the result of a gradation from one colour to a second or even third colour. This can be achieved because, essentially, you are laying down brushstrokes both horizontally and at an angle.

At the top of the paper, paint a single-colour graded wash of Winsor blue, as described in Method 2. While the paper is still wet, change to a similar mix of cadmium red for the lower part. Because everything is still wet, it should be relatively easy to work the colours into one another. Gravity ensures that the blue will flow down into the red, but it will be necessary to paint the red upwards, slightly, into the blue. Don't worry if it looks a little messy to start with, as the colours will even themselves out as they dry.

MULTICOLOUR GRADED WASH
In this example, French ultramarine was applied first as a graded wash, then cadmium red was added to it, while it was still wet, and I then worked the two colours into each other. Note that you will need to work quickly for this to be successful – the minute the wash starts drying, you run the risk of creating backruns.

WET-ON-DRY AND WET-IN-WET

When you apply paint to paper, irrespective of what stage a painting is at, the appearance of your brushstroke will depend upon one major factor: whether the surface it is being applied to is dry or damp. In these two extracts from 'Sunrise over Otley' (the full painting can be seen on page 22), the difference is clearly illustrated.

In the extract right, the trees have been painted on to a dry surface therefore the edges of the resulting brushstrokes are hard. This is an example of wet-on-dry.

In the extract left, the clouds have been painted on to a damp surface; the resulting colours have been allowed to fuse together, creating soft edges throughout. This is an example of wet-in-wet.

WET-IN-WET WASH

At any time during the production of a watercolour painting, when paint is allowed to mix in a free fusion of colours on the paper, you can be said to be working wet-in-wet. In some ways, the graded wash is a wet-in-wet wash, although its horizontal, linear properties make it a very orderly and carefully planned activity. A good wet-in-wet wash, however, should have an unruly, unpredictability about it. Quite simply: when colours are allowed to blend and bleed together in this fashion, things happen that can never be planned!

To me, wet-in-wet washes characterize the whole spirit of watercolour. Freedom of expression, the thrill of not quite knowing what a wash is going to look like until its last moments of drying – these are qualities that you must thrive on if you're going to get the most out of the medium. However, with unpredictability comes uncertainty, and you may have to learn to embrace those aspects of the medium over which you have very little control.

1 Ensure your painting board is at an angle of 15–30 degrees, then thoroughly wet the paper with a wash of clean water. Working quickly, paint a rich mix of cadmium yellow on to the wet paper in sweeping, random brushstrokes, from the top down. Don't paint the yellow any lower than halfway down the paper, since the effects of gravity will ensure that it continues to work long after its application, soaking gradually into the clear wash.

2 Time is an important factor in the success of a wet-in-wet wash. As its name implies, whatever colours you use, it is crucial that you keep the paper wet at all times (the soaking at the beginning needs to be thorough). Apply a medium mix of cadmium red to the wash while the cadmium yellow is still wet, roughly emulating the shapes made by the yellow, but not obliterating it – the red will also continue soaking into the wash, so give it plenty of room to do so.

3 Finally, apply a small amount of French ultramarine in the same carefree spirit with which, hopefully, you applied the other two colours. Again, give it plenty of room to soak into the wash, and don't obliterate the red.

TRANSPARENT WASH

This brings me to the fourth, and arguably the most important, of the basic watercolour washes, the transparent wash. Combined with identifying tonal values and understanding their importance in the structure of paintings, there should be a healthy respect for one of the major properties of watercolour itself – transparency!

Transparent washes are weak washes that, when overlaid on top of each other, produce increasingly darker tones. This is using the transparency of the medium at its best – only very rarely should watercolour washes be applied so heavily as to not allow previously applied brushmarks to show through.

Any of the basic washes featured on previous pages can be used as a starting point for a simple landscape, the natural progression from which would be to start overlaying simple shapes, such as mountains and hills.

By laying simple transparent washes of the same intensity on top of each other, the illusion of depth and distance can be achieved without the necessity of re-mixing.

It is crucial that the density of colour in the foreground mountain shapes is allowed to intensify subtly and by virtue of simply being an accumulation of layers built up on top of each other, not by altering the intensity of the colour mixes.

Before tackling the mountains below, experiment by overlaying simple bands of the same mix of French ultramarine on top of each other.

Practise painting transparent washes similar to these. They don't have to be exactly the same, and you can create different mountain ranges, based on the Alps or Rockies perhaps, or whisk up something from your own imagination.

Whatever you do, note how important it is to keep each subsequent mountain within the bounds of the previous shape, otherwise you'll end up with mountains made of glass.

COMBINING WET-IN-WET AND TRANSPARENT WASHES

The process of laying weak, identical washes on top of each other was used to create this simple landscape, using a wet-in-wet wash as a base upon which to work. The three transparent washes are of French ultramarine; the mix was only altered when painting in and building the and foreground detail last of all, by adding a small amount of burnt umber to darken it.

Always remember that the lightest, brightest part of your painting is the white of the paper, which should be allowed to show through your washes as you build them up. Never be in too much of a hurry to get your darkest tones down; it is far better to build them up gradually, using the transparency of the medium to its full effect. Apart from anything else, applying light washes carefully and allowing the tones to build up gradually gives the painter a greater sense of control over their work. With watercolour, it's always easier to make something darker than lighter.

TRANSPARENT AND OPAQUE

To me, transparent washes represent the pinnacle of watercolour technique. Oil painters may have the ability to paint light tones on to dark tones and the luxury of being able to rework parts of their painting simply by scraping it off and starting again, but watercolourists have something that oil painters can only dream about – transparency!

SUNRISE OVER OTLEY 17 x 56cm (10 x 22in)
The low-lying mist gives a magical mystical quality. To create the mist, I kept that portion of the paper damp at all times to ensure soft edges. I used wet-in-wet in the clouds, and painted the trees wet-on-dry for hard edges.

Concerning tone

DRAWING

This is a simple demonstration of how easy it is to represent different tones in pencil. In fact, because pencil, by its very nature, uses only one colour, it's a great medium with which to teach yourself the importance of tone, and to see things in terms of light and dark. When it comes to successful drawing and painting, tone is absolutely everything!

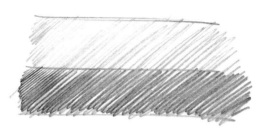

Draw out four horizontal lines to create three bands of equal size. Shade in the bottom two bands using an even shading pattern, then just the bottom band (over the top of the previous shading) to produce a similar result to that shown here.

Now repeat the exercise, only this time, think mountains.

RELATIVE VALUES

It is important to understand what tonal values of objects are and how their appearance is often affected by other, adjacent objects of different, contrasting tones. In this first example, the foreground rocks and the left-hand trees appear dark against a light, unshaded background. In this second example, the sketch has been developed further. By considerably darkening the background trees (on the right), the foreground rocks now appear light in tone, relatively speaking. In a similar manner, the background trees, too, now appear light once the sky has been shaded in with a dark tone.

The importance of tonal values

Tone refers to the lightness or darkness of an object and is far more important than the colours you use, in as much as it can make or break a painting.

A painting may have lots of colours within it, but if they are all of the same tonal value, removing the colour would turn the subject into one large, single smudge. You can create a painting with only one or two colours (and some paintings benefit enormously from this), but if the contrasts between the lights and darks are not well defined, the painting will be substantially weakened because of it.

If necessary, you should exaggerate or emphasize tones where the subject is inherently tonally bland. On a dull day, you might even need to engineer such contrasts from the very beginning.

PERSPECTIVE

Tone also plays a part in helping to create the illusion of depth. In addition to linear perspective (when objects recede and appear smaller in size as they get further

ABOVE WASDALE 17 x 26cm (7 x 10in)
By the wonders of modern technology, it has been possible to completely remove the colour information in this painting (above), allowing us to view it purely in terms of its tonal values. The illusion of depth has been created by keeping the distant hills light in tone, while the foreground rocks have been made more prominent, and forthright, by being painted in darker, richer colours.

RELATIVE TONES

In these two patterns, which circle is lighter in tone? The answer is that both are exactly the same, but one appears lighter because the square surrounding it is much darker than the other. What this simple optical illusion teaches is that tone is relative. In watercolour, because you can only work from light to dark, objects can't be made lighter by painting them lighter: you can only make them appear lighter by making adjacent objects darker.

away), artists employ aerial perspective. This is where washes depicting distant objects are painted cooler in hue and lighter in tone, to further enhance the illusion of depth and space.

CONTRAST

The next time you have a minute to spare, try contemplating a world without contrast. It doesn't matter where you are: one good long look about you should be enough to convince you that our visual perception of the world about us owes a greater proportion of itself to tone than any other single thing, and this is probably the one element in pictorial creation that can make or break a painting.

It is an indisputable fact that everyone sees the world about him or her slightly differently. It would also be true to say that everyone who picks up a brush applies paint differently. This means that if you were to present several dozen artists with the same identical subject, and ask them to paint it, you would end up with several dozen completely different interpretations of that same subject.

Given this, whether your personal style is inherently bold and rich, or light and delicate, your painting must recognize contrast. Look for the lights and darks within the subject, and make them work for your painting.

COUNTERCHANGE

When you take time out to observe your environment, look again at those things we all tend to take for granted. Look closely at how tones change according to what they are set up against: for instance, a tall building may look white at its base, but as your eyes travel its length towards the top you notice how, if it is a bright day, the upper floors appear dark against the light of the sky. On a different day, however, when the sky is stormy and threatening rain, those same upper floors of that same building, lit by a last glimpse of sun, might appear light against a dark sky, while the lower floors descend into gloom.

This visual phenomenon is known as counterchange, and is characterized by one object or surface graduating from a light to a dark tone, while an adjacent object or surface graduates in the opposite direction.

As with the mountains, the tree appears to graduate from light to dark, even though, in reality, it is unlikely to differ so greatly. This manipulation, however blatant, is perfectly acceptable to maintain clear definition between objects within a composition.

BUILDINGS

If there is one word guaranteed to induce sweaty palms and dizziness in students (second only to 'fee'), it is 'perspective'. Although referring to it in hushed tones as 'the P word' may go some way to pretending it's something that can be avoided, it is inevitable that you are going to have to confront it – particularly if you are going to tackle buildings.

Many of the problems associated with perspective stem from the fact that we tend to take so much for granted. It isn't until we try to draw any subject that we realize just how relevant the old maxim, 'Draw what you see and not what you know is there', really is.

PERSPECTIVE: SQUARES AND CUBES

 This exercise shows how to transform three simple, two-dimensional square shapes into three-dimensional-looking cubes. Remember, it is important to draw freehand, without the aid of any form of straight edge. Don't be worried if your shapes look a little rough at the edges (we all look like that from time to time).

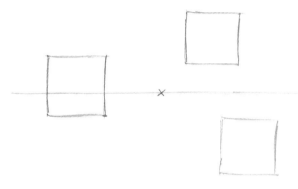

1 Begin by drawing a straight, horizontal line. This is your eye-level line. Add three square shapes, one above the line, one below, and one straddling the line. Once you've done that, draw a cross in the centre of the line.

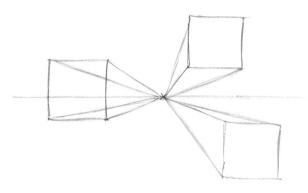

2 Join each of the four corners of the left-hand square to the cross using straight lines – this has the effect of making the square look transparent. Imagine the remaining two squares as solid surfaces, and only join up the closest three of their four corners.

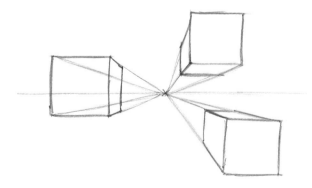

3 To transform your squares into cubes, draw in their furthest edges. Be sure to foreshorten the sides – the distance between the new vertical edges on the sides must appear smaller than those facing us. It is important to notice that the maximum number of surfaces you can ever see on a cube is three (and there are only two on the left-hand cube here).

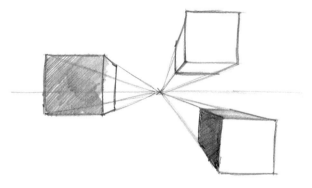

4 Now shade in the cubes. At this point, the absolute correctness of tones is relatively unimportant. In reality, the direction of light has a great impact on which surfaces should appear darkest and lightest. For the purposes of this exercise, however, it is more important to try and create as smooth a covering as possible. The objects' perspective lines appear to converge at a single point (known as a vanishing point or VP), which is known as one-point perspective.

TWO-POINT PERSPECTIVE

In the last example, the objects all have one surface facing directly towards us, with their resulting perspective lines converging at a single point. However, what happens if those same shapes are rotated, so that no flat surface points directly towards us? Two vanishing points are created, as shown in the following exercise.

MOVING ON

Apply this simple array of vanishing points and perspective lines to more complex shapes of your own design (a house perhaps). Again, note how the top edges of surfaces above eye level come down to meet the vanishing points, while those below come upwards to meet them.

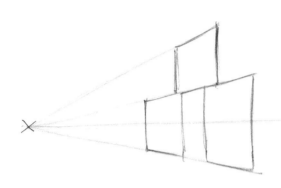

1 Begin by drawing a straight, horizontal line, with two crosses at either end. To draw the shapes as in the example, start with the nearest vertical edge to you.

2 Follow exactly the same rules as in the previous exercises, only this time connect each corner to both vanishing points. Remember that these are cubes, and the top and bottom edges of each surface run parallel to each other, so they share the same vanishing point. All the vertical lines remain vertical – they just appear smaller the further away they are.

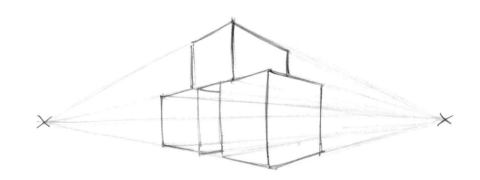

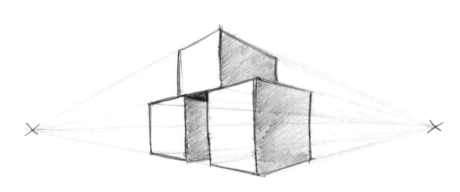

3 A simple, plain shading pattern is all that is required to complete the drawing (note the darker tone on the underside of the top cube).

A SIMPLE BARN: DRAWING

From the exercises on the previous pages, it requires only a short leap to turn a simple square shape into something a little more ambitious, such as a building.

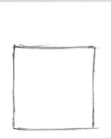 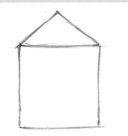

1 Begin by drawing a square in freehand (no rulers allowed).

2 Add a simple roof.

 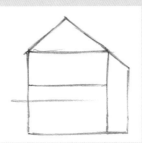

3 To add perspective to the barn, you need to be able to see more than just the facing surface. To do this, extend the line of the roof down one side (in this case, the right-hand side) for just a short way.

4 To add a small extension, draw two horizontal lines, parallel to each other and the base of the building, to the end of the barn, extending the lower line.

 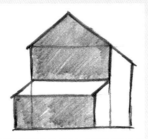

5 Connect all the lines, and your sketch should now be looking vaguely like a building. If it isn't, check that your uprights are correctly drawn vertical, your horizontal lines are indeed horizontal, and that all lines that should be running parallel to each other are doing so.

6 Finish off your sketch by shading in all the surfaces directly facing you. Although simplified, the result is extremely effective, and is how I would actually draw such a building on a sketching trip.

DRAWING

Using the methods described in the exercise on the left, now try your hand at drawing a slightly more ambitious version of a barn.

Here, a simple composition has been created by adding a road and a fence. The building has been enhanced by adding a small window to the extension, and a door and windows to its side-on surface. Note the addition of lines to the lean-to's roof to suggest slates, and the small amount of shading along the edge of the main roof to suggest a slight overhang.

In this version of the subject, the visual details have been taken that little bit further, with the inclusion of stones by the side of the road and some stonework on the barn wall. Try the sketch yourself. Note how accuracy is not always necessary – in fact, this particular subject benefits greatly by being a little on the worn side.

WATERCOLOUR

The natural progression from producing a sketch is to consider how it might be developed into a painting. For this exercise, I used 300gsm (140lb) Arches Rough watercolour paper.

1 Begin by drawing out the basic outline of the barn and road using a 2B pencil. Keep your lines light so that they can be modified if you make a mistake, and, tempting though it may be, don't add any more detail than that shown – the pencil marks are intended to be nothing more than just a guide, defining and positioning the size and shape of items within the work area.

PLANNING

This is the point, early on in the planning stages of a painting, at which mistakes can still be easily rectified. Always take your time over the initial planning of work. Think things through and, if necessary, draw other sketches to help your decision-making. Further on in the book, the process of developing paintings and thinking through ideas using pencil sketches is described in greater detail. Even though this is a relatively simple exercise, the basic principles still remain the same.

2 Paint a light, weak mix of burnt umber over the whole of the barn, taking care to leave the little window as untouched paper. Even though part of the building is going to be in the shade, it's a good idea to paint the entire thing as if in sunlight, and lay the shadow colour over the top of it. This is using the transparency of the medium to the full. One alternative to overlapping washes in this way is to paint areas of paper individually in a mosaic-like fashion, a process known as open wash.

3 Apply a weak mix of French ultramarine as evenly as possible to the shaded surfaces of the barn and along the edge of the roof. If the ultramarine appears too 'blue', add a tiny amount of burnt umber to the mix, 'neutralizing' the ultramarine and creating a subtle blue/grey colour. If this mix proves difficult, an alternative is to use Payne's grey or neutral tint.

4 When everything is dry, paint in the door and windows, using a rich, dark mix of burnt umber and French ultramarine. The roof colour was created here using burnt umber and cadmium red, and the green of the grass is cadmium yellow and Winsor blue.

5 The stones on the walls of the barn were painted in burnt umber, and several were randomly selected and made to appear darker by repainting them after they had dried.
The sky was kept simple, so as not to detract from the main focal point. It consists of a single, plain wash of weak Winsor blue applied to a dry surface, carefully leaving areas untouched to suggest cloud shapes.

RANDOM PATTERNS

Creating random patterns of shapes and lines is one of the hardest things to get right in landscape. The natural world about us, however orderly it might appear at first glance, is a heaving mass of random events. Re-creating the random appearance of such things takes a little practice, and many paintings suffer from just looking too tidy.

In this example, the random appearance of the stonework on the barn, and the stones on, and by the side of, the road is crucial. Always take advantage of unplanned brushstrokes and areas of drybrush, where the paint has run out part-way through the stroke and the smoothness has been broken up. It's these moments that can transform a subject into something quite remarkable. The trick is to pretend you meant to do it in the first place.

FINISHING TOUCHES

As with all things, it's the little finishing touches that often make a painting stand out from the crowd. Adding detail and texture describes an object beyond simply saying how big it is and what colour it is.

Detail and texture indicate what material an object is constructed from and what it might feel like to the touch, bringing added realism to a painting. On a note of caution, however, always take care to ensure that these sorts of details are not overdone. It is almost always preferable to slightly understate things, leaving a few gaps for the viewer's imagination to fill in. In this way, the viewer 'interacts' with the painting and has a stake in it. It is for this reason that very often some of the simplest, most under-worked paintings have the most impact.

Always ask yourself, therefore, is this brushstroke necessary? If in doubt, leave it out.

Project: The old barn

Old farm buildings are always attractive to the landscape artist. As time goes on, however, it's highly likely that many such structures will disappear from the landscape, only to be replaced by newer, probably shinier, alternatives.

As paintings from yesteryear have become important historical records of a time long since passed, so we should bestow the same status on anything that we represent in watercolour today. Over the years, I've seen old buildings slowly absorbed into, then swallowed up by suburban growth. If you know of one near you and you haven't yet painted it, do it today, while there's still time!

SKETCHING

1 I began by drawing out the basic outline first, taking extra care over the perspective. Because the barn is receding, the lines of the roof slope gently down towards some unseen vanishing point, and the far left-hand corner appears lower than the nearest. These basic rules of perspective are easy to get wrong when sketching on site. Closing one eye can help to 'flatten' the view, and holding a pencil up to the object can help in assessing the correct angles. I slightly exaggerated the overhang of the left-hand tree to help strengthen the links between parts of the scene. It is important for the collection of individual shapes and lines that constitute a painting to intersect and relate to each other in a visually interesting way. This is the classic landscape format, which allows artists to capture a view in the same way that they look at it naturally. Here, the horizon line is halfway up the drawing, but it can be easily moved, depending on the viewpoint, without much change to the effect.

PLANNING THROUGH SKETCHES

A pencil sketch is a means to an end. It is a place to think your subject through. A place to make all your mistakes. Whatever your source material, explore your subject as thoroughly as possible through sketching. Graphite is considerably cheaper than paint; cartridge paper is cheaper than watercolour paper. If you can think of sketches in terms of being your preliminary notes, you are well on the way to creating better paintings. I feel more comfortable with a subject once I've sketched it in pencil; that little bit more familiar.

2 Once I was happy with the basic outline, I added details and shaded in the window at this end of the barn, even though this was not the case in the source photograph. Feel free to take liberties if you think they will help improve the painting in some way. I drew in several lines to help get the perspective right. Having gone to all the trouble of drawing the outer shape correctly, it would be a shame to then have the lines of stones sloping at an unnatural angle.

Red slate

3 To finish the drawing part, I concentrated on drawing in the shadows, first those cast by the overhanging tree, then the darker tone beneath the overhang of the roof. I used a combination of drawing and shading in the stones with drawing the gaps between the stones, and added a note to remind me what material the roof was made out of (that's not to say I wouldn't change it when I came to paint it, but it gave me a hint of the colour it should be). I exaggerated the dark tone of the background trees (to the right of the building), to emphasize the light surface of the barn's end wall.

PAINTING

4 Using the pencil sketch as a guide, I began by drawing out the basic outline of the barn with a light, weak mix of burnt umber. I almost always plan out a watercolour using paint rather than pencil, but if you are unsure about this, plan your subject out in pencil – but keep the lines light so that they may be erased on completion.

5 I then applied an initial wet-in-wet wash of cadmium yellow and Winsor blue to loosely define which areas of the painting were sky and which were to be summer foliage.

KEEPING A FRESH EYE

It's important to keep an overview of your work at all times. For this reason, I recommend taking lots of breaks when painting. I reckon that 30 minutes painting time, followed by a break, then repeated until the work is complete, is about right. Walk away from your painting regularly, and try to see it with a fresh eye. It's easier to spot errors that way (another way to see your painting in a fresh light is to look at it reflected in a hand-held mirror).

6 When the wet-in-wet wash had dried, I added a light wash of burnt umber and cadmium yellow to the walls of the barn, and a mix of cadmium red and burnt umber to the roof. Because this was a rural farm building, I made sure that the stones in the walls had a certain random quality, suggesting age and wear. Resisting the temptation to paint every single stone, I tried to ensure that they all went in roughly the same direction.

CHECKING THE TONES

It's worth stopping a moment to look at the tonal qualities of the painting at this point. If, by the wonders of technology, all the colour information were to be removed, it can be seen instantly that, despite the fact that about five different colours have been used at this point, they are all of roughly the same tone.

Never underestimate the importance of tone. Because this is only the mid-point of the painting, the lack of tonal range is not an issue. From here on, however, much thought must be given to developing the contrasts in the composition if there is to be any chance of success.

7 Next, I added blue/grey shadows throughout the painting. In addition to helping to bring a painting to life, shadows also add extra definition to the three-dimensional shape of objects. I particularly concentrated on the shadows cast across the roof of the barn, while reducing those touching the nearest corner, to avoid confusion (while a whole mass of dappled shadows can be appealing to look at, they must be controlled when it comes to painting them). I used negative painting in a few places to create a smattering of grass detail. This is preferable to using masking fluid, as the result is likely to be more spontaneous and natural-looking.

8 I added the darkest tones using a dark, rich mix of burnt umber and French ultramarine, then mixed a mid-tone green from cadmium yellow and French ultramarine and added it in small amounts to the undersides of the foliage. By randomly darkening the odd few stones, I introduced a little variation to the wall. Finally, feeling that the barn doors in the source photograph were a little too tidy, I enlarged the gap between the two main doors and added a little rot to their bottom edge. Tidiness can be fatal to a painting such as this, so you should always be on the lookout for opportunities to add that little extra.

FINAL THOUGHTS

What to include and exclude in a composition is, of course, up to the individual. Fortunately, it's one of the things that makes us all different. Another artist might feel the need to spend more time over the roof or add extra detail to the undergrowth in the foreground. In this example, I've deliberately tried to keep the foreground down to a minimum, although I'm reasonably satisfied that the suggestion of long, tangled greenery has been achieved.

The decision of how much to show of, or how much detail to paint in the light, blue/grey trees visible in the background wash was left up until the last minute, as was the decision not to add anything further to the light area between the end of the barn and the overhanging tree. I felt the air of mystery it created, along with a clear, unambiguous focal point, more than justified my slightly guilty sense of laziness at the time.

TREES

Trees are an important 'key' to the landscape. Adorned with full foliage (summer greens or autumn golds) or stark and winter-bare, they provide a visual clue to what time of year your painting depicts.

I've broken this chapter down into three sections. While both winter and summer trees are dealt with in some detail in the latter two sections, this first section seems like a good time, using simple tree sketches, to introduce a few basic rules to help you begin to understand the complexities of painting design.

BASIC COMPOSITION

When it comes down to it, a painting is just a series of shapes and lines of varying tone and colour, applied to a blank piece of paper. How you arrange those shapes and lines is important, and however spontaneous and free your approach to the activity is, there must be a satisfactory, underlying structure. If there isn't, then the vision you are hoping to convey, and the response you are hoping to provoke, may be severely compromised. The art of picture organization is known as composition.

The rules of composition are many and varied, and although some may be bent, to disregard the more basic principles is to invite disaster – break the rules at your peril!

TWO SUBJECTS In the example, left, the trees are identical in size and shape, and also mirror each other's vertical position on the paper.

Moving them closer together and reducing the size of one creates a stronger, more interesting composition.

Lightening the tone of the smaller tree and giving it a cooler colour helps to create depth.

FOCAL POINT The tree is too central. Moving it slightly to one side is far more preferable. Never place your focal point dead in the centre, or too near the outer edge of the paper.

LEADING THE EYE The addition of a road in this final example of the same scene helps to draw the eye to the focal point, as does the line of distant trees. A small amount of detail has been applied to the foreground, which until now has been flat and featureless. Another compositional trick would be to darken the extreme foreground, to lead the eye from the dark into the light.

COMPOSITION CHECKLIST

Focal point

Every painting should have only one focal point: one main object of interest. The rest of the composition should be designed to draw the eye in towards the focal point and strengthen it, not compete against it. More than one focal point weakens the overall composition.

Tonal contrast

This is the strategic positioning of light values against dark values. Capitalize upon such occurrences by exaggerating them, and if there are no such contrasts in the subject, create them. A painting with no contrasting tonal values will be uninteresting and lacking in depth.

Over-all balance

Don't make your painting off balance by placing too many closely grouped objects or too much detail on one side of the paper. Strong horizontal lines that effectively divide the painting into two should be broken up by vertical lines or objects that pull it together.

Graduation

If you have a large area where nothing is happening, try introducing some form of graduation to create interest. This could be a gradual change from, say, a warm colour to a cool colour or a light value to a dark value. It can even be a change from a rough-textured surface to a smooth surface.

Variation and alteration

These are necessary to avoid boredom or repetition. For example, a line of trees should ideally not be all of the same height and regimentally spaced, but of varying or alternating heights and colours.

Coincidences

Try to avoid alignments that weaken your painting. Coincidences where the vertical or horizontal lines of objects coincide exactly can seriously weaken your composition. Be aware of the possibility of such occurrences, and look to engineer the composition so as to avoid them wherever possible.

TWO SOLUTIONS In this example (right), the composition suffers by the top of the tree coinciding with the line of the background hill. In the picture below, the height of the tree has been raised to break up the line of the hills. In the picture below right, the hill has been raised and the tree moved slightly.

AVOIDING REPETITION This evenly spaced line of identical-looking trees is vastly improved by varying their height and the spaces between them.

IMPROVING THE CONTRAST Removing the colour information is sufficient to see how tonally bland the subject is, despite all the colours used. Both monochromatic examples below show how contrast might be improved by exaggerating the tonal contrasts.

Winter trees

There are few things in the landscape more fascinating than a winter tree. While spring is a time of reassurance, the appearance of new buds signifying the start of another year's growth, winter seems to bring out a curious combination of vulnerability and strength in trees; they are so bare in their skeletal form and yet have the ability to withstand almost anything and everything that the elements might throw at them.

As always, the best way to approach drawing winter trees is by breaking them down into their most simple form.

DRAWING SIMPLE SHAPES

 Before looking at winter trees in any detail, you can use the technique shown on page 14 to improve accuracy, and apply it to a simple tree.

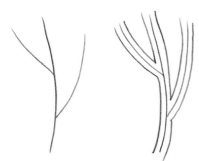

1 Draw the initial shape as a simple guide. Then draw the outer shape of the tree, keeping the lines as parallel to one another as possible.

2 Shade in one side of the tree, using a plain shading pattern up the main trunk and the left-hand branch, and a graded shading pattern on the upper portion of the trunk and the right-hand branch.

3 Draw a more natural-looking version in freehand. It doesn't matter if the lines come out a little lumpy or wobbly, as this all adds to the realism of the drawing. Note that the main tree trunk should appear to get slightly narrower the higher up you go – take care not to reduce its width too dramatically, however, or it'll look wrong.

ADDING DETAILS

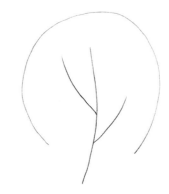

1 To draw a more complex tree, start with the same simple design as before, and draw an inverted horseshoe shape around it, to represent the furthest point that any subsequent branches will reach.

2 Add the rest of the branches. These should each be a reproduction of the first, basic design, becoming smaller in size as you go along the branches. No two smaller branches must sprout from the same point on a larger branch.

3 Again adapt the simple design into a freehand tree. With practice, you should be able to create a nicely rounded tree without the aid of the horseshoe guide. Note that all the branches curl upwards slightly, including those lower down, which start out by pointing downwards.

WATERCOLOUR

1 As with the sketch opposite, begin with the main trunk and largest branches. Here, the lightest tone is a mix of burnt umber and cadmium yellow. Apply a darker tone of burnt umber and French ultramarine to the left-hand side while the first wash is still wet, allowing it to bleed across the width of the trunk, to suggest and emphasize its shape. Work more dark tone into the still-damp surface to create contours and texture.

2 Switch to a smaller brush and gradually work towards the finer branches, drawing them out to the tree's furthest reaches; a fine pencil line drawn as a guide may be of help here.

PEELING BARK It's a good idea to make sketches of bark, both in pencil and watercolour. The knowledge you gain from such close observation will improve your work, even if such details are not always visible on the trees you paint.

To achieve the illusion of peeling bark, all you need to do is apply the same rule as with stones. Painting a very dark, rich tone up against a line on the bark will 'lift' it, giving the impression that it

is standing proud of its surroundings. In the example below, a liberal amount of drybrush has formed the basis of the tree, to which increasing dark tones have been applied. Small backruns have also been encouraged, since they also contribute to the impression of texture.

BARK AND TEXTURE Look closely at the bark of a tree and you'll wonder why you never looked that closely before now – the surface is often pitted and cracked in unpredictable ways. For this reason, backruns, drybrush and other 'imperfections' that you cannot ever plan should be encouraged. Trees that look a little rough at the edges always look so much better than smooth, 'designer' specimens!

Many pigments will granulate on application. This, allied to the properties of rough paper, always helps to create surface texture.

SHAPES OF TREES

Trees come in all shapes and sizes. In an ideal world, the best way to improve your drawing and painting of trees would be to study them as thoroughly as possible. I've known people who can spot a species of tree just from looking at a fallen branch. They're able to tell me its name, whether it's deciduous or evergreen, where it originates from and how you would order one from a list of Latin names in a mail-order catalogue.

I suspect that my flippancy actually belies a jealousy of such people's greater knowledge. The fact is, I'm always promising myself that I'll read up on trees to gain that little bit extra understanding – and never do. Shame on me! The truth is, I give very little thought to the name of a tree, and instead try very hard just to understand the shape, size and colour of a tree in the context of the composition I'm working on. This is actually a far cry from my very early work, when downright laziness would cause me to simply draw or paint in a 'stock' tree.

As a general rule, trees fall into the following categories: round (ash, birch, horse chestnut); oval (oak); tall/slim (poplar); and triangular/'pointed' (fir, spruce, cedar, larch).

Adding depth

Creating depth in a painting is just one of the many challenges we are faced with when it comes to producing a convincing visual statement. In real life, we see things three-dimensionally, and can perceive spaces between objects, breadth-wise, far more readily. Trees, in particular, grow outwards in all directions and should therefore, wherever possible, be shown to have branches reaching towards us. By not considering this, trees run the risk of looking flat.

Here, then, are two methods suitable for creating depth in your trees, when working in both pencil and watercolour.

DRAWING

 To avoid your trees looking flat and two-dimensional, sketch them in two tones. Make the first part of the sketch a rough interpretation in a light tone (which could stand alone as a tree partially hidden by mist); to provide a three-dimensional quality with added depth, draw a darker, sharper layer over.

WATERCOLOUR

The same effect can be produced in watercolour by painting the tree in two stages. Apply the first wash using a weak mix of French ultramarine and burnt umber, and allow it to dry completely. Then add a second layer, using a darker, richer version of the same mix. Keep the brushstrokes rough around the base of the tree, to suggest ivy at the bottom of the trunk.

'FUZZY' TREES

This example features two special effects associated with bare winter trees. The first I like to call 'fuzzy' trees (below left and inset). Useful for emphasizing depth by making background trees appear out of focus, this technique requires you to paint the trees on to the initial wet-in-wet wash while it is still damp.

The second effect can be seen along the tips of the smallest branches (below right) – by graduating their colour to a warm mix of cadmium yellow and cadmium red, they appear to be caught in the light of the sun. This effect is a particular favourite of mine, offering the opportunity to introduce added warmth to what might otherwise be a cold scene, and to avoid uninspiring silhouettes.

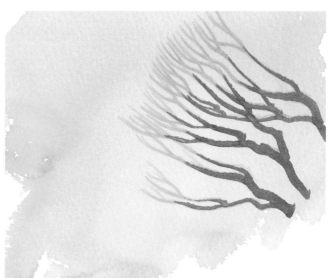

Take care not to apply the trees too early, or they may disappear into the wash. Also, don't stop in mid-branch, or you will create unsightly blobs, not dissimilar to monkey-puzzle trees (however, if monkey-puzzle trees are what you're after, this is the answer).

WINTER SUNRISE, KILBURN 17 × 56cm (7 × 22in)
Both effects described here are featured in this simple winter scene. The background trees were painted in first, as part of the initial wet-in-wet wash. Timing is crucial if you want your trees to have just the right amount of 'fuzziness': too early, and your brushstrokes will either disappear into the wash or appear too broad; too late, and your brushstrokes will be falling on to a dry surface and will appear hard-edged. Note how the smallest branches of the foreground tree curve upwards slightly at the end. This is important if you want to avoid your tree looking dead.

Project: Winter trees

Of all natural subjects, majestic trees top my list of all-time favourites, and none more so than the extraordinary skeletal specimens that are revealed in winter. It's easy to be daunted by the masses of intertwining branches that constitute the form of the winter tree, so take time out to study them. If there is more than one tree, try and identify which branches belong to which one, and concentrate your attentions initially on the overall outer shapes. Simplification has to be the key here.

SKETCHING

1 When sketching bare winter trees, it is a good idea to begin by drawing the main trunk first, before attacking the finer branches. I started at the base and then worked upwards. In this example, the most noticeable thing about the two trees featured is the apparent difference in width between their main, central trunks. This, of course, is because the left-hand tree is further away, but simple things like this are easy to overlook. The other main difference is that only a very small portion of the nearer tree can be seen, while the distant tree is almost entirely visible.

2 I shaded in the dark side of the foreground tree, and drew in the path – in the source photograph, the path is visible but is not immediately apparent; but I decided that if it were more prominent, it could serve as a useful compositional tool, helping to draw the eye into the scene.

3 To finish the distant tree, I added the smaller branches. It's always worth taking a little extra time to familiarize yourself with the particular tree you're working on, rather than falling into the easy trap of lazy sketching – all trees are quite different and deserve to be recognized as individual specimens.

Remember: branches always curl up slightly at the end, unless they're dead.

4 I next drew the darkest tones, paying particular attention to the detail on the foreground tree. Note the gradual shading employed on the base of the trunk to accentuate it and bring it forward. I added the shadows, so prevalent in the scene, last of all, and found myself improvising slightly with the suggestion of rocks and stones on the path, because I was thinking ahead as to how the drawing might be transposed into a painting.

PAINTING

 5 Using a light, weak mix of burnt umber, I plotted the main elements of the scene on to watercolour paper. I paid careful attention to the correct positions and proportions of the trees, without adding too much detail at this early stage. I particularly liked the way that the lower branches of the foreground tree 'framed' the background tree.

6 For the sky, I used an initial, wet-in-wet wash of Winsor blue, French ultramarine and alizarin crimson; and for the ground I applied a mix of cadmium yellow and burnt umber (because this is a winter scene, greens would not be in keeping).

7 Next, I painted in the background tree with a light mix of burnt umber and French ultramarine, and gave the foreground tree a graded wash of French ultramarine, burnt umber and alizarin crimson, to give the illusion of shape. With a subject like this, any accidental backruns or random, untouched highlights should be welcomed, since they all add extra texture to the tree.

8 I applied a blue/grey mix of French ultramarine and burnt umber to cast shadows across the ground, and used the same mix, slightly diluted, for very distant objects, such as the pale background trees and bushes. It's important for these objects to remain weak so that they don't compete with the foreground. It's worth remembering that a wintry tree caught in the sun casts shadows not only along the ground, but also upon other parts of itself – in this case, the main tree trunk. Being slightly curved, these shadows also help to further accentuate the roundness of the tree trunk.

9 Gradually I added darker tones, mixed from French ultramarine and burnt umber, to the foreground tree to further increase its prominence in the overall composition, and to create added realism to its shape. I extended the highlights along the tops of both the left-hand protruding branches slightly into the main trunk, and painted the right-hand protrusion to make it look as if it were growing out of the front of the trunk, and not its side; this increased the illusion of the tree being a 'real' object in three-dimensional space. Avoid the 'totem-pole' effect, where branches all appear to grow outwards from a two-dimensional pole.

FINAL THOUGHTS

Winter trees can be quite a major challenge on a sketching trip. If many are grouped together, sorting out which branches belong to which can be quite a headache. As with trees in full foliage, you should first whittle them down in number slightly, decide which are the most important, and use these as your starting point.

In this demonstration, trees at different distances have all been given slightly different tones and colours: the lightest, coolest colours have been given to the most distant objects, whilst the darkest, richest colours have been reserved for the most prominent, foreground object. This effect is known as aerial perspective, and is a formidable weapon in the artist's armoury. If necessary, you may have to exaggerate or even engineer the differing colours and tones from scratch, to gain maximum benefit for your composition.

I debated long and hard whether or not to keep the seat in the painting, and finally decided that it was one of those simple elements that could give the scene a surprising lift. So, ultimately, I'm pleased I left it in.

10 Finally I painted in the finest branches of both trees, then used a medium mix of burnt umber on the footpath, deliberately leaving a few random highlights suitable for turning into rocks and stones (a carefully placed brushmark directly alongside any white highlight instantly becomes a stone). I used a little negative painting at the very base of the foreground tree in order to create a few blades of grass, and then applied a second, slightly darker blue/grey to the distant bush immediately behind the main tree trunk, to reduce its otherwise flat appearance.

Summer trees

For me, summer trees symbolize light and shade. As well as providing life and the illusion of movement to a scene, the shadows they cast also offer excellent opportunities to define the contours of the ground from which they have grown. How does one adequately capture the myriad of colours and shapes? Where does one end and another begin?

The sight of many trees caught in bright sunlight can be magical, and the only really effective way to convey that same illusive quality is to keep the whole thing as loose as possible. Don't feel you have to reproduce every single tree in the view – more importantly, look for the direction of flow in their combined shapes.

WORKING IN ORDER

In general, when drawing summer trees, it's always advisable to work on the foliage first, then the branches. It's much easier that way to make the branches seem to disappear into the foliage and reappear further up. I often find that squinting at a tree helps to reduce it down to a more simplified form. Attracting strange looks from passers-by is the least of my worries.

1 The easiest way to approach a summer tree in full foliage is to reduce it to its simplest form. In this example, suggest the areas of foliage as simple circular shapes of differing sizes, which are joined together by branches as described on previous pages.

2 These simple shapes can then be developed into something more tree-like by redefining their outer edges, in a rougher form. The shapes appear to curl up, because the unseen branches within the foliage tend to grow that way.

3 Finally, fill out the trunk and branches, either on the sketch you're working on, or produce a freehand sketch, as shown here.

TREES IN THE DISTANCE

Trees viewed from a distance are unlikely to have very much detail. When sketching trees, the top example here usually suffices. It tells you how many trees there are and how they are distributed. The middle and bottom examples take the information that little bit further, with the inclusion of trunks and branches. In the middle sketch, the foliage was shaded in first, and the dark trunks and branches were added afterwards.

Often, however, tree trunks appear light against the darker tones of the lower areas of foliage. To create these, in the bottom sketch I shaded the trees in a similar manner to the top sketch, and carefully applied a dark shading to the base, working around the tree trunks in a 'negative' drawing manner.

The watercolour equivalent of a similar line of trees is shown below. The lightest tones should be dropped into the background wash while it is still damp (not wet), followed almost immediately by the mid-tones.

PAINTING ON DRY WASHES

The daunting task of painting a tree in full summer foliage is best tackled in three stages, and can be simplified by being broken down into three tones: light (cadmium yellow and Winsor blue), mid (cadmium yellow and French ultramarine) and dark (the mid-tone plus burnt umber and more French ultramarine). Each wash was allowed to dry before the next tone was applied.

Note how the darker tones have been kept to one side to suggest the direction of light. When painting in the trunk and branches, these must make some sense, so think about the underlying structure of the tree. Don't overdo them: less is more.

TREES ON LOCH LOMOND 17 × 26cm (7 × 10in)
In this painting, the breakdown of tones can clearly be seen. I often leave lightest tones as cadmium yellow to keep things light and fresh.

USING DRYBRUSH

Of course, there's more than one way to paint a tree. These two examples were painted using a drybrush technique. Always give some thought to how much detail you actually need to show in your painting. The left-hand tree is a single colour, with the trunk and branches added while it is still damp. This would be perfectly adequate for a background or middle-distance tree. The right-hand example was produced in exactly the same way, but had a second layer added to it, thus increasing the foliage detail.

Project: Summer trees

Almost without exception, things look more tantalizing at the opposite ends of the day. Shadows grow long, the throngs of human visitors thin out, and an air of mystery descends. This is a great time for artists with an eye for the potential subject for a painting. In this exercise, a scene packed with the foliage of summer, the trees are well defined by extremes of contrasting tones.

SKETCHING

 1 When sketching trees in full summer foliage, you should define their outer shapes first. Here, I effectively mapped out the whole scene, breaking the objects down into their simplest, most basic forms. Note how the top edge of the right-hand wall, because it coincides with the eye level, appears to be more or less flat and horizontal.

2 Having reduced the scene to its most simple form, I added the tonal values using a mixture of plain and gradual shading. Because this was a sketch, precision was not important. Its purpose was to familiarize myself with the subject and decide where the lightest and darkest tones were, and how they related to each other. The fact that the lights and darks alternate throughout was to be crucial to the ultimate success or failure of the final painting. Light tones set against other light tones could compromise and weaken the composition.

3 I completed the sketch by adding a second, darker tone to the main, central tree in order to accentuate the smaller tree in front of it, and then redefined the outer edge of the topmost foliage using a darker, sharpened pencil point. This is often necessary when a good deal of shading has been undertaken, because pencil lines tend to get smudged by the edge of your hand. Only when all the varying tones had been added did I sketch in the fine details. I added a few light pencil strokes to the road to suggest shadows and to provide a hint as to where the light was coming from.

PAINTING

4 To re-create the scene in paint, I began by reproducing a simplified version on watercolour paper, using a pale burnt umber. I prefer this to using pencil, as it often seems less intrusive. If you would rather use pencil, work with a 2B and keep your pencil lines down to a minimum so they can be removed later on.

5 I next applied wet-in-wet washes, using Winsor blue for the sky and cadmium yellow for the foliage and over the whole tree area, even where it was ultimately going to be in the shade. Since the main purpose of this first wash is to roughly define areas of sky and areas of foliage (almost as a kind of underpainting), I allowed both colours to bleed into one another to create a result that had a deliberately loose and spontaneous feel.

6 Once the initial wet-in-wet washes had thoroughly dried, I applied a medium-strength green, mixed from cadmium yellow and Winsor blue, to the trees. Applying it to the areas of shadow emphasized the lighter undertone. In watercolour, you can't paint light tones – you can only make tones seem lighter by darkening tones adjacent to them.

7 Next, I added a blue-grey mix of French ultramarine to the line of background trees, painting the wash into the foliage to create a ragged edge. This is a simple form of negative painting. An alternative would have been to use masking fluid, but I prefer to live a little more dangerously in a bid to create a more spontaneous approach. I applied a graded wash of French ultramarine, burnt umber and alizarin crimson to the opposite stone wall, again carefully painting around the undergrowth at its base.

8 I added a mid-tone green, mixed from cadmium yellow and French ultramarine, to the areas of foliage. It was important not to obliterate any of the lighter tones I had already painted, and to keep in mind where the light was coming from.

At this point, the road was still untouched paper. It's better to err on the side of caution and leave some areas untouched, otherwise you run the risk of making it unnecessarily dull.

9 Shadows help to bring a painting to life. Here, I used French ultramarine and burnt umber to create a blue/grey ideal for painting shadows, rocks, stone and many other natural features. For me, these two colours have very special qualities, and I probably use them more than any other colours throughout my work. Starting with French ultramarine and adding burnt umber to it in very small amounts, you'll discover that they have the effect of neutralizing each other. Don't try it the other way around (starting with burnt umber), because this doesn't work quite so well, the burnt umber being the more dominant colour.

10 Finally, I added the darkest tones (mixed from burnt umber and French ultramarine) to the scene, including the branches of the trees and a smattering of detail on the wall. I also applied a small amount of very dark, but graduated, tone to the base of the trees where they meet the top of the wall, to help accentuate the walls and make them stand out almost three-dimensionally. To finish, I added a small amount of burnt umber to the sides of the road, to give it a little colour and to suggest texture in the form of small stones.

FINAL THOUGHTS

To summarize: when sketching and painting summer trees, always start with the foliage first, and add the tree trunk and branches later (but don't overdo it). Break foliage down into two or three tones (light, mid and dark). A useful way to help you see a simplified version is to squint at it.

In the finished painting, you can see how the composition has been simplified even more than the sketch. The part of the road that reappeared beyond the brow of the hill has been taken out completely. Always remember: if you feel a composition will be stronger for it – do it. In this case, I didn't feel the reappearance of the road contributed anything significant to the composition, so out it went. If anything, taking it out has added a slight sense of mystery to the scene – where does that road go?

SKIES

The renowned landscape artist Rowland Hilder used to say 'Paint a sky a day'. While I would agree this is an excellent idea if you can fit it into your daily schedule, I would say if you can't do that, then Steven Spielberg's 'Watch the skies' is probably a good second best. The more you study skies, the better your watercolour skies will become.

Unless we're specifically looking for a sky to paint, then we often don't notice it unless it's particularly spectacular (and if it is that spectacular, then, like me, you've probably thought, 'If I paint it like that, no one's going to believe me anyway!'). There has to be a balance. A good sky will bring mood and atmosphere to a composition, but it shouldn't be quite so overpowering as to detract from whatever else is happening visually.

THE SCAFELL RANGE, FROM BOW FELL Detail
Despite the painting being largely geological in content, it's the sky that tends to dominate the composition, providing a tantalizing glimpse of England's highest mountain range. Anyone who has ventured into these parts will be familiar with that breathtaking moment when the clouds part and present the vista that you've been praying for all day. This is a combination sky painted in two stages (a wet-in-wet stage, for the soft edges, followed by a wet-on-dry stage for the hard-edged patches of blue) as described on page 64.

COLLECTING AND USING SKIES

One of the most wonderful things about skies is the fact that they can be imported into any painting. It is a good idea, therefore, to get into the habit of 'collecting' skies wherever and whenever you can. An interesting sky may present itself at any time, so a camera is always handy to have near at hand, whether you are relaxing in the garden or are loading the week's groceries in the car park.

When you are out sketching, skies should be given top priority. Always try to be aware of them and capture them in the form of photographs, pencil sketches or watercolour sketches. The main challenge of capturing skies in sketch form is that the most visually interesting ones often don't stick around for long, so you need to work fast. Don't worry if you miss it, though; there'll almost certainly be another one along in a minute!

Tending to take up one of the largest areas on the paper and probably being the first wash you apply, the sky is often responsible for setting the overall mood of a painting. Allow yourself the luxury, therefore, of using skies in a creative way. Think about what mood you want to convey in your painting, and produce your sky accordingly. It could be that the scene you are wanting to paint has an interesting sky anyway; it may be the one element that attracted you to it. In the same way, a relatively bland scene can be transformed into something quite extraordinary, simply by being lit in a dramatic or atmospheric way.

CIRCLES AND CLOUDS

This exercise involves creating a sky using simple circle shapes as a basis for clouds. While all clouds are different, they tend to follow the general pattern of being larger at one end, according to the direction in which they're moving, and appearing rather flat along their base.

1 To draw accurate circles, it's a good idea to set your hand moving in a circular motion above the paper, pencil poised, before making a mark. Develop your four overlapping circles.

2 To develop the shape, draw over and accentuate the clouds' overall outline.

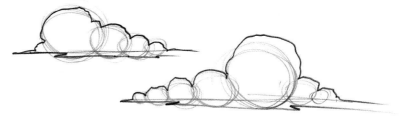

3 Create a highlight by drawing an inner line and shading the cloud with a plain shading pattern.

CLOUDS AND LIGHT

It is vital that the shadows on clouds are on the same side, in order to make sense of where the light is coming from.

1 Repeat the last exercise, only this time begin with two sets of interlocking circles, the second (right-hand) shape being more irregular in appearance.

2 This time, however, when you draw around the outer edge, follow the circles as before, but attempt to make them more 'cloud-like' (that is, not quite so circular in appearance).

3 Next, attempt this example, first using the simple circle and line shapes as a guide, then repeat the exercise freehand, without the use of any guidelines. Complete the picture by shading in the sky and clouds, taking care to leave a highlight along their top edge.

4 Finally, practise designing your own simple sky sketches. Take the time to go outside and look at some real skies *in situ*. Have a go at drawing what you see, using the basic techniques described in this chapter. The more you observe skies, the better equipped you will be to draw and paint them. Many poorly painted skies suffer from the artist simply not having taken the time to study them.

Wet-on-dry

If you've spent any time at all looking at skies, you will have realized that no two are ever the same. Not only that, the preconception that the sky is always blue and all clouds are fluffy couldn't be further from the truth. In this section, I'm going to concentrate on the concept of hard edges. In watercolour terms, this means painting them wet-on-dry – the careful layering of washes on top of each other.

SKETCHING FOR WET-ON-DRY

Before painting a sky, it's often a good idea to plan it out in the form of a preparatory sketch beforehand.

Here, I have used a plain line drawing to define the main groups of cloud shapes. Remember that clouds near the top of the paper should appear larger and bulkier than those nearer the bottom edge, which should, in turn, be smaller and more horizontal in appearance. To fully familiarize yourself with the sky, first shade in the clouds to ascertain where the light is coming from, and where the highlights are likely to be, then redraw the outer edges of the clouds with a heavier line to finish.

SIMPLE WASH AND LIFTED-OUT CLOUDS

Nine times out of ten, a simple wet-in-wet or graded wash is all that is required to produce a satisfactory sky. If you want to depict cloud shapes, however, the simplest method is by lifting out the shapes from a still-damp wash with a screwed-up sheet of dry tissue paper.

Keep rotating the tissue as you work, to avoid re-applying the paint to the paper, and work quickly – as soon as the wash has dried off, no further clouds can be lifted out.

This method is fine, provided it is applied in a subtle manner and not over-used. Generally speaking, uncluttered skies are best, and clouds should only be added if they contribute to the overall composition, and do not hinder it.

PAINTING WET-ON-DRY

 A wet-on-dry sky is one where light washes, allowed to dry fully between each application, are overlaid on top of each other, creating hard edges throughout. In this example, the blue of the sky (painted in Winsor blue) has been applied to clean, dry, untouched paper.

The suggestion of soft or broken edges has been created by drawing the brush along on its side, when most of the paint has been used up (drybrush).

When the Winsor blue has dried thoroughly, a light, blue/grey mix of French ultramarine and burnt umber has been applied to the underside of the clouds, taking care to leave a highlight along their top edge.

Despite the variations of shaded tone applied to the sketch, I've deliberately kept the watercolour version of the sky as a simple two-stage example. If the subject demands it, however, the application of a third, slightly darker tone may be worth considering.

This example of a sky painted entirely wet-on-dry displays a cloud inversion, where the lighter part of the clouds is on their undersides due to the newly risen sun being so low in the sky. Although it is not my favourite method of painting skies, I almost always approach a subject as complex as this one using the wet-on-dry method. In this case the blue, graduating to yellow, was applied first, leaving all the clouds as untouched highlights, ready to take the warmer colour once dry.

Wet-in-wet

The exact opposite to wet-on-dry, a wet-in-wet sky is produced as one multicoloured wash where colours are applied to a wet surface that is not allowed to completely dry out until the very end. The result is a sky where there are no hard edges to be seen anywhere, only soft ones.

As synonymous with traditional watercolour technique as wet-in-wet skies have become, it should be remembered that artists such as Turner were recognizing the importance of creating mood within a painting, and that the sky, for all its vastness, provided that vital, key element.

The examples on these pages represent two completely different moods but differ only in the mood they convey, mainly thanks to the choice of colours. While the sunset scene on this page (below) painted in warm, golden hues mixed from cadmium yellow and cadmium red, suggests a mood of quiet tranquillity, its counterpart opposite is far from tranquil.

For wet-in-wet, choose your colours carefully and, as a general rule, try to keep them down to a maximum of three in number.

SKETCHING A WET-IN-WET SKY

Although there is no direct pencil sketch equivalent of a wet-in-wet sky, this does not mean it can't be visualized and planned in much the same manner as described in the previous section. An initial layer of plain shading (no line drawing) is used to define the general layout of the sky (top). Then, a further layer of shading has been applied to the clouds, effectively bulking them out and giving the illusion of shape (above).

SUNSET AT MARAZION

28 x 38cm (11 x 15in)
This view of St Michael's Mount off the coast of Cornwall is a particular favourite of mine. You never know for certain how a wet-in-wet wash is going to develop; here, the simple, warm hues fused together in a pleasing way. I postponed the decision of whether or not to introduce a little more detail to the Mount until the last minute, finally settling on the simple in preference to the unnecessarily complex. I think that the resulting mysterious quality was worth all the deliberation.

A PATH THROUGH THE PEAT GROUGHS

Pencil sketch and finished painting (top) 28 × 38cm (11 × 15in)
The Kinder Scout plateau can be a bewildering and highly dangerous
place to the unwary walker. In such a featureless terrain, you can't
help but notice the angry clouds as they scud across your path.

PAINTING A WET-IN-WET SKY

Because successful wet-in-wet requires you to work relatively quickly, it's a good idea to have your colours ready
mixed. Because of the unpredictability of this particular
method, it's best not to have too rigid an idea of how you
would like the sky to finish up, but far better just to accept
whatever happens and pretend you really meant to do it in
the first place.

Allow yourself to live a little dangerously, but don't be
tempted to apply dark colours too early on. With wet-in-
wet, you never really know what it's going to look like until
the very last moment of drying. It's worth remembering,
however, that while it is wet, paint can still be pushed
around. Speed is the essence, but give yourself breathing
space by not committing to anything too concrete. Enjoy it,
get angry with it, but don't give up until it's starting to dry
off – that's the danger zone, when the damp sheen on the
paper's surface is no longer visible. That's when you stop,
and wait and see what it looks like in five minutes' time.
Don't fiddle – if you do, you'll pay for it!

Two-stage combination sky

This is the method by which I tend to produce the majority of my skies. Before putting paint to paper, you should take the time to look closely at the sky you are attempting to produce, and decide where the hard edges are, and where the soft edges are.

1 Once you are clear in your own mind as to how the sky is divided, the first stage of painting is the wet-in-wet stage, concentrating solely on the soft edges. In this example, the shadowy undersides of the clouds are where the soft edges are to be found, so first paint an all-over wash of clean water, then add a blue/grey mix of French ultramarine and burnt umber. Take care not to apply the paint while the paper is too wet, or the brushstrokes are likely to diffuse and spread too much to control.

2 When your first wash has thoroughly dried, apply the blue of the sky to the dry surface, creating hard edges. Take care to leave a highlight along the tops of the clouds, and use a second brush, damp with clean water, to selectively soften parts of the blue wash to create a little variation. Manipulate the shapes and flow of the clouds to achieve maximum realism. Remember: skies are an integral part of the overall composition, so you should take care to avoid one of the most common pitfalls, the pattern-like repetition of shapes.

NEGATIVE SKY DRAWING

In the same way that light tones can be effectively created in watercolour through the adjacent positioning of counteracting dark tones, the same effect can be produced in pencil. Careful examination of this sky should reveal how it was developed in two distinct stages. The first is to establish the major areas of light and shade.

In the second stage, the further application of increasingly dark shading layers gives rise to further, subtle details within its darkest regions. The most important thing is to keep the horizontal band of cloud in the foreground as prominent as possible by retaining the untouched white of the paper. The faint cloud details along the bottom edge were applied last.

LIFTING OUT THE SUN'S RAYS

This effect is most common in both the early and last hours of sunlight, and during stormy periods of sunshine and showers. When the conditions are just right, a veritable light show created by the rays of the sun apparently bursting out from the layers of cloud near the horizon, can be a visually dazzling phenomenon.

SUNBURST ON LOCH LOYNE 13 × 35cm (5 × 14in)
This scene is typical of the Scottish Highlands, where random and sudden breaks in the cloud provide a constantly changing mood.

To create the effect in watercolour, first paint the sky 'straight', then carefully lift out the pigment with a damp stencil brush, using two straight-edged pieces of card as a 'mask' to create the impression of rays. It helps if you have several pairs of hands, but if you're only in possession of the standard one, then, sticking the card down with masking tape can help to hold it steady while you scrub. Although a stencil brush is ideal for lifting out paint in this way, it should be implemented carefully so as not to damage the surface of the paper. With practice, you can lighten an area of wash in a subtle manner, without removing it completely.

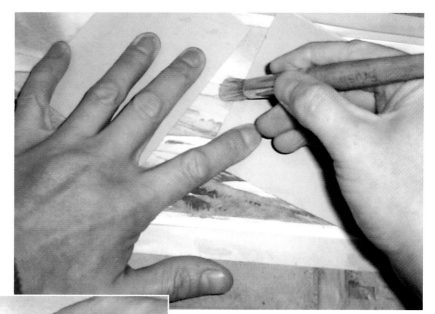

Take care, also, with positioning the rays. By putting in this effect you are essentially pinpointing the position of the sun, so they must make sense. Here I used a piece of tissue paper. Highlights should appear to get only slightly wider, and should all point in roughly the same direction.

Project: The Rock of Cashel

The source photo of this impressive complex of ancient buildings in the Republic of Ireland, which towers 60m (200ft) above its surroundings, features what could only be described as an unremarkable sky, but despite the nice weather at the time of viewing, I couldn't help but see the overall scene with anything other than a spectacular sky as a backdrop.

SKETCHING

1 I began the sketch by drawing out the main elements of the scene using a single pencil outline. There is a small amount of over-sketching along the top edge of the outer wall, resulting in 'furry lines', caused by trying to get the angle right. It's often far better to correct things by over-sketching than getting into the trap of constantly correcting mistakes with an eraser, which can become counter-productive. Provided that you've not drawn things too heavily, 'furry lines' can often result in a more informative sketch. I identified the foreground mass of exposed rocks and tussocky grass as a useful, integral part of the design that could help to strengthen the overall composition.

2 Next, I applied a layer of plain shading, with the sole purpose of clearly defining the areas of light and dark tones. This is an ideal time to look out for unfortunate visual coincidences and 'magical alignments'. For instance, it is vitally important that the dividing line on the tall tower does not fall exactly in line with the corner on the wall. If that corner were to be moved to the left by just a tiny amount, it would, along with the dark tone on the rock in the foreground, split the painting cleanly into two halves horizontally.

3 I completed the sketch by re-drawing the outer lines with a bold pencil line. The windows were added to the buildings using simple, single pencil lines, and a little stonework detail was added to the outer wall. I also applied a second layer of shading to parts of the scene, creating a third, slightly darker tone. Taking hints from the cloud shapes in the source photo, I drew out the sky design, looking at how it might fit into the composition. It is important for all the separate elements to 'lock' together in a satisfactory manner, and not seem to be disconnected in any way – here, the sky, the cluster of buildings and the foreground rocks all relate to each other, so that the composition works towards drawing the eye in towards the focal point.

PAINTING

4 I began the painting with the sky, laying down a loose, wet-in-wet wash of French ultramarine, burnt umber and alizarin crimson, and applied a small amount of cadmium yellow to the lower edge of the sky. The UFO-shaped object that hovers above the main left-hand building was an accident. After debating what to do about it, I decided it would be best left alone, and worked into the design later on. This was a case of damage limitation, as any attempt at softening the highlight and blending it into the surrounding wash could potentially have had disastrous results. It is often far better just to leave things be.

5 Once the initial wash was dry, I applied a light mix of burnt umber and cadmium yellow to all of the buildings and walls, followed by a blue/grey shadow colour using the same mix I'd used for the sky. The grass was a mix of Winsor blue, cadmium yellow and burnt umber.

6 When the initial blocks of colour had established the shapes and contours of the rocks and grass, I used no fewer than five layers of increasing tonal intensity to build them up.

Layer 1
Burnt umber and cadmium yellow

Layer 2
French ultramarine and burnt umber

Layer 3
French ultramarine, burnt umber and alizarin crimson (medium mix)

Layer 4
French ultramarine, burnt umber and alizarin crimson (darker mix)

Layer 5
French ultramarine and burnt umber (darkest tones)

7 I completed the painting by applying a light, weak mix of Winsor blue (cerulean blue is also good for this) to the lightest part of this two-stage, combination sky, to suggest a dramatic break in the clouds. I allowed the blue brushstrokes to create hard edges along the tops of the clouds, and created soft edges along the undersides by carefully softening them with a brush half-loaded with clean water – bringing too much water to an earlier wash can result in unsightly backruns, while applying too much pressure with the brush can disturb the original wash. Although dabbing pigment off with a tissue should be largely avoided, it may be necessary to lightly touch the softened-off area to stop the Winsor blue bleeding into it and creating yet another hard edge.

FINAL THOUGHTS

Despite the fact that the sky takes up only a small proportion of the overall composition, its impact is undeniable. Never be afraid to take risks with skies – if you have a promising subject, think carefully about how you would like to see it lit; perhaps think of lighting a painting as being very similar to lighting a scene in a play or a movie. In this example, a nice day has been transformed into a moody one, simply by changing its sky. While the core subject remains relatively unchanged, the ambience created by the inclusion of a sky that looks like it might just be raining on you any minute makes all the difference.

Of course, this painting represents only one of an infinite variety of ways in which it might be painted. These two further examples illustrate how different the scene looks and how the atmosphere can be subtly altered when painted with a different sky.

RIVERS AND WATER

Water is a constant presence in the landscape: rivers, lakes, the sea, even in non-aquatic subjects, water is there – the weather often sees to that. So, at some point, it is inevitable that you will have to sketch or paint it. And this means learning to understand its properties and its effects on objects associated with it. Primarily, I'm referring to reflections.

UNDERSTANDING REFLECTIONS

Since the science of reflections, involving angles and mathematical equations, can be more than a little daunting to us mere mortals, who just want to paint them, in this section I'm going to try to simplify them and offer a few simple rules, which should help to keep your water looking like water.

SKETCHING

 In the first sketch, the view is direct at the bridge. Because of this, the underside of the arch is only barely visible. A figure, standing on the bank beyond the bridge, can clearly be seen reflected in the water. The most important rule of all can be made here: any point on an object must reflect directly below itself, irrespective of where it is viewed from.

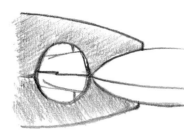

In all the previous illustrations, the water has been kept completely calm, resulting in convenient mirror-like reflections. In nature, however, since rivers and streams are constantly on the move, waves and ripples are created, which distort and break up reflections. This is because ripples and waves have two, tilted surfaces, both of which are reflecting objects, but in slightly different directions.

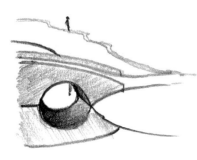

When the same bridge is viewed from above, the figure is still reflected directly below itself. Now the underside of the arch can be seen – but only in its reflection. This is because objects appear in their reflections as you would see them from the surface of the water, where the reflection is located.

Note how the wall of the archway appears to get lighter near the water's surface. This is because a small amount of light is reflected up from the water at this point, resulting in this graduation in tone.

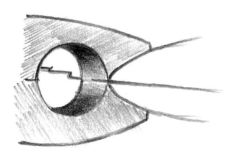

In this more realistic example, priority has been given to showing the flow of the river, over any necessity for accuracy in the reflections. When sketching water, draw only what you see and try to capture the basic essence of the scene.

PAINTING

 In the simple example on the right, the inside of the boat is not visible in its reflection. The mast appears to break up because the foremost ripples are reflecting from two surfaces – one facing the mast, and one facing towards a lighter sky, somewhere above and behind the viewpoint.

Ripples also obey the laws of perspective by appearing to get larger the closer they are to the viewer, smaller and more tightly packed together the closer they are to the object.

RIVERSIDE GRAZING 17 x 26cm (7 x 10in)
This tranquil scene, depicting the River Wharfe in the heart of the Yorkshire Dales, has been made all the more so by limiting the water-surface detail to an absolute minimum. The slightly uninterested and unenergetic sheep contribute to the mood.

Reflections and shadows

 Reflections are often mistakenly painted like shadows. Their properties, although similar in visual terms, are quite different: while shadows, cast by an object, fall obliquely away in the opposite direction to the source of light, reflections always appear directly below the object. This rule applies wherever it is you happen to be viewing the object from.

Of course, reflections differ in appearance according to the surface of the water in question. Still water, such as a lake, is likely to produce sharp, almost mirror-like reflections, while fast-moving or disturbed water (in the case of rivers or open water) will produce broken or distorted reflections. Since water has no colour of its own (except for maybe a little local colour from sediment), you should consider how an object is going to appear in its reflection. Generally speaking, reflections appear slightly darker in tone than the original object, but the actual appearance must fit in with the overall composition.

STILL WATER

Of all the subjects containing water, completely still water (that which has very little or no surface movement at all) is the one that makes me slightly nervous. Very often, photographs depicting such a scene show reflections so perfect that you're not immediately certain which way up they should be viewed. One reason painting such a scene can be so uncomfortable is that painting

BARE HOUSE, GRASSINGTON MOOR 36 × 56cm (14 × 22in)
Puddles are an extremely useful compositional device. In addition to helping to set a mood — their presence indicative of a recent rainstorm, or suggesting the onset of a thaw after snow, as depicted here — they provide a useful excuse to bring colours from the sky down into the lower portion of a painting, essentially linking the top and bottom halves of a composition together.

water seems to be nothing more than a straight, if inverted, repetition of the view.

My recommended solution to this problem is two-fold. First, don't try to repeat the view too clearly or sharply – depicting the water in the form of a wet-in-wet wash is probably the best way to do this, drawing colours down from the view above, as you use them. Alternatively, the water can be painted wet-on-dry at the same time as painting the view, bringing the colours down as you use them and applying a light, weak 'glaze' of, say, burnt umber, over it after it has dried, to suggest what is known as 'local colour' (this would be caused by the presence of sediment from the bed of the water, or from the surrounding landscape; peat, for instance).

Finally, I would recommend introducing a little surface movement by running a damp brush across it horizontally, or carefully scratching out a narrow highlight somewhere in the middle distance. This would be perfectly acceptable even on the stillest of days – a light breeze, disturbing the surface.

In this example of 'still water', I painted the lake first as a wet-in-wet wash, then added the reflections of the tree trunks and foliage after it had dried.

WET-ON-DRY AND WET-IN-WET

In the example on the left, the water was painted entirely wet-on-dry. The colours used above the waterline are brought down into the water and built up piece by piece in a mosaic-like pattern. In the example on the right, the water has been painted wet-in-wet. The colours used above the waterline are brought down into the water and allowed to bleed into one another, diffusing the reflections and creating an overall softer effect than the first wet-on-dry version.

Because the water is flowing, as opposed to still, surface movement is suggested by the inclusion of ripples: those in the foreground were lifted out after the wet-in-wet wash had dried, using a stencil brush and cardboard mask. The highlights in the middle distance were carefully scratched out with the side of a scalpel blade.

Whichever method you employ, the most important thing to remember is that an object's reflection should appear directly below it, not at an angle in the way that its shadow would appear.

The sea

From a distance, waves appear as highlights near the shore, and as slightly deeper-toned, soft-edged lines further out to sea. Note how important it is to maintain random spacing between the waves. In the gentle shoreline scene below, the rolling waves contribute to the flow of the land.

What the two paintings at the bottom of this page have in common is an emphasis on movement: waves are, after all, the product of a great natural force coming to bear on a vulnerable coastline.

COUNTY KERRY 13 x 35cm (5 x 14in)
The west coast of Ireland is as magical and ethereal a place as it is claimed to be. This view, from the southern coast of the Ring of Kerry peninsula, is typical of an area festooned with small islands and curved bays.

Breaking waves can be produced in two ways. These waves were painted wet-in-wet. The challenge when using this method is in keeping the area of soft spray damp throughout the painting procedure.

The second method of painting waves, demonstrated here, involves using masking fluid. This gives you the freedom to paint the background and foreground details after first protecting the area of spray created by the breaking wave.

WAVES

Rolling and breaking waves tend to follow a simple pattern, and both drawing and painting them is largely a matter of creating shape and movement through accurate tonal work. Notice how, in the watercolour, the sea is not always blue; the lighter tones are mixed from Winsor blue, cadmium yellow and burnt umber.

This simple watercolour exercise has been built up stage by stage on a dry surface. After I painted the sky, I depicted the distant sea using tightly packed horizontal bands of Winsor blue. I then added the foreground waves, painted with a blue/grey mix of French ultramarine and burnt umber, taking care to place them at a slight angle (for greater visual interest) and to leave an untouched highlight along their tops, to suggest the breaking foam.

In the foreground, the water's surface is dominated by the patterns of foam. I warmed the mix up slightly with the addition of a small amount of alizarin crimson. These foam patterns are useful to the composition, helping to draw the eye inwards towards the closest, most prominent wave.

Finally, I applied a narrow line of dark tone, mixed from French ultramarine and burnt umber, to the top of the wave, just below the highlight, to help suggest its curved shape.

Project: Highland stream

White water is water so fast-flowing, usually over rocks and down a steep incline, that its turbulent surface appears irregular and almost solid. The most important thing to remember is that its appearance is dictated by the shapes of the rocks just beneath its surface, so thinking about how those rocks might look without water is one of the keys to determining how the river should look in full flow.

SKETCHING

1 I began the sketch by positioning the main elements of the scene: where are the most prominent foreground rocks situated? How do they relate to the background trees? It was important to start simple and not be tempted to draw in too many details too early on.

2 As I shaded in the rocks, introducing a little detail into those in the foreground, I made those furthest away seem more tightly packed together and horizontal in appearance. The spaces between the rocks represented water, and I used a few carefully applied light pencil strokes to define where the major drops were.

3 The foliage of the background trees was next. I concentrated on shading in the darkest tones, leaving the tall, straight trunks as highlights. I added further shading in the dark areas to suggest barely visible trees deeper in the wood. When shading areas like this, it can be necessary to redefine the edges of objects by drawing over them. Here, I redefined the left-hand edge of the trees and a couple of the tall tree trunks at the top.

4 I completed the sketch by drawing in the line of fir trees visible along the distant hill, and redefining the foreground rocks. It's important in a scene like this to know exactly where the darkest tones are. Don't worry about over-exaggerating things when drawing: the purpose of the sketch is to familiarize yourself with what's there, and how it all relates to each other. If you compare it with the photograph, you can clearly see how I edited the subject by reducing the number of rocks and including only those that made a contribution to the overall composition.

PAINTING

5 I began the painting by drawing it out using a light, weak burnt umber. Although I included the single, bare tree in the centre, I didn't develop it in later stages. This was because, throughout the painting process, I remained undecided on whether I liked it there or not. I'm not usually this indecisive, but on this occasion I simply couldn't make up my mind.

6 I next applied an initial wet-in-wet wash using Winsor blue for the sky and cadmium yellow for the foliage. The yellow wasn't an accurate representation of trees at this point, more a sort of 'underpainting', where the yellow merely set the scene. I also applied the left-hand hillside to the damp surface, giving it a soft, out-of-focus look. Nothing was set in stone yet, so I could easily have repainted the hill to give it a sharp edge, but on reflection, I preferred the softer finish, which added depth to the scene.

7 When the initial washes had dried, I began painting in the rocks, using burnt umber. 'Spotting' the brushstrokes at the base of the foreground rocks helped to create the impression of foaming water. This is by far the hardest part of a scene like this – introducing a random element to make it all look natural and to avoid creating patterns of repetitive shapes. This is 'negative painting', so the gaps between the dabs of paint represent drops of water on the rocks.

8 I used a mid-tone green, mixed from cadmium yellow, Winsor blue and burnt umber, to develop the foliage of the trees.

9 To develop the trees even further, I used an increasingly dark mix of the cadmium yellow/Winsor blue/burnt umber combination. I used the negative painting technique around the light trunks to the right, and then applied darker tones to the darkest trunks (on the left-hand edge of the wood), concentrating these along the undersides of the foliage.

10 For the water, which so far had been untouched paper, I used French ultramarine with a little burnt umber added to tone it down slightly. Water always benefits from having its detail kept to an absolute minimum.

CHOOSING BLUES

Winsor blue is a Winsor & Newton colour, available in artists' quality only, which comes in two variations, red shade or green shade. I always recommend the red shade because it's warmer and mixes well with cadmium yellow (another staple colour). If you are working with student-quality paints, or prefer to use those from a different manufacturer, the closest equivalent is phthalo blue (Winsor & Newton student colour) or Prussian blue (any other brand).

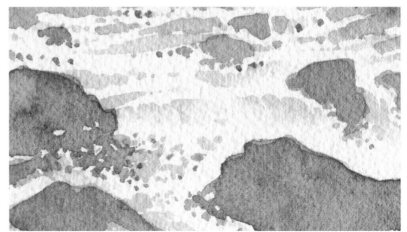

11 Think about why water looks the way it does, and note how it appears light along the top of each drop, where the light hits it, and light at the bottom of the drop, where the water becomes a mass of turbulent foam. I used the brushstrokes to signify the direction of flow, and softened the brushstrokes along the bottom edge to emphasize the spray.

12 Finally, I added the darkest tones, primarily to the undersides of the rocks, their rich severity acting in stark contrast against the brightest whites of the crashing waters. This contrast of extreme light tones against dark tones is something I come back to time and time again: its importance makes it worth repeating. I then applied a hint of cadmium yellow and burnt umber to the top edges of each fall – streams in full spate like this can churn up silt and sediment from below, making an almost milky consistency. I compromised on the hillside: although it retains the soft, misty quality created by the initial wet-in-wet wash, I decided that the very top edge of a distant forest, just peeping over the horizon, would help to balance up the rest of the composition.

FINAL THOUGHTS

To the landscape painter, water is a gift. It provides numerous ways in which to extend and disperse the available light, and gives a means of linking different parts of a painting together and emphasizing and exaggerating the mood you want to convey.

Here, the cascading water is made all the more dramatic by the extreme contrasts inherent in the subject. Deliberately exaggerating the darkest tones at the base of the rocks made the white of the water spray appear to be even brighter.

Remember: in watercolour, tones are relative. The brightest, lightest part of any painting is the untouched surface of the paper itself (white paint straight from the tube will always seem quite dull by comparison). You can't make things lighter in watercolour; you can only make them appear lighter by darkening any adjacent tones.

SNOW

There is something innately irresistible about a snow scene. Maybe it's seeing the landscape at its most challenging (in all respects), or perhaps it's because the preponderance of white paper and stark contrasts in tone make it the kind of composition that can be produced quickly, and with few brushtrokes. It's possible, of course, that snow scenes just make me a little nostalgic for childhood winters that always seemed so much more fun and 'wintery' than those I've experienced as an adult.

NEGATIVE SHAPES

I remember being given an exercise to do in art at school, where the instructions were, 'Don't draw the object; draw the spaces around the object.' This is the essence of negative painting. I would go a little further and say that much of what occurs in painting happens as a direct result of something else. A simple pencil line or brushstroke might represent an object, but our curiosity prompts us to ask questions regarding where it is situated and how it relates to other objects. Our eyes, therefore, instinctively fall to the immediate surroundings. By crafting a painting carefully, you can make a secondary point of interest as important as the first.

It's not until you attempt to draw snow that you realize just how close the relationship between pencil and watercolour is. In neither media can you directly produce light tones – you can only create the illusion of, and control, light tones by placing them next to dark tones.

1 To reproduce this simple winter scene yourself, begin by leaving the outline of the wall.

2 Next, overlay shading patterns of gradually darkening tone.

3 Add the details of the fence and grasses, as well as darkening the scene with shading.

This example was produced solely with the use of shading (no solid lines), but it may help you to lightly draw the scene out first.

THE IMPORTANCE OF SHADOWS

A shadow tells us as much about the surface upon which it is being cast as the object casting the shadow itself. In the case of snow, the importance of shadows is even greater. Without them, snow lacks any definition, or visual information pertaining to its shape or form.

A single shadow is enough to show how flat, or otherwise, the ground is.

In this example (left), the shadows tell us the ground is completely flat.

While in this example, the snow is made to appear lumpy and real by curving the shadows cast by the fence.

Further simple brushstrokes have been added to this final example in order to expand the scene. Note how even the little blades of winter grass produce curved shadows.

SNOW SCENES – WARM OR COLD?

Just because snow is cold, this doesn't mean that a snow scene has to speak in degrees below zero. In many ways, the juxtaposition of warm against cold is an irresistible one – hence the many snow scenes I've painted over the years. Of course there are going to be times when the full force of winter is the primary objective – cold, angry, moody skies convey a winter in all its life-threatening reality. However, I like to paint winter scenes with a touch of warmth, conveying those magical moments when the light tricks us into believing that a walk in the snow might be a good idea. For me, these are the moments worthy of a watercolour.

Drawing and painting snow is a joy because subjects are reduced to their simplest forms: contrasts are never more apparent, and light and dark tones are never more obvious and easy to define. Trees stand out dark and proud against fields of virgin snow, and buildings peek out, slightly embarrassed by the featureless burden that threatens to hide them completely. This lack of detail, though a godsend in some respects, can cause compositional problems not encountered elsewhere, as a featureless expanse of snow looks flat and two-dimensional without any definition.

WINTER GLOW, BUTTERMERE
28 x 38cm (11 x 15in)
When painting snow a creative use of shadows comes in handy, and the shadows may even have to be exaggerated and emphasized.

FALLING SNOW – SALT GLAZING

A great way to create a falling-snow effect is to use a technique called salt glazing. Begin by laying down a wet-in-wet wash. Wait a few moments for the wash to soak in and dry slightly, then liberally sprinkle sea salt across the surface of the paper and wait for it to dry. You can use ordinary table salt, but sea salt, in the form of flakes, is better because its grains are more irregular in shape.

As well as being ideal for falling snow, this technique is also good for creating any sort of texture. Its big selling point is its random element. Snow can also be lifted out of a wash using tissue or a rag over the end of a brush handle, but it's much harder to create a random, natural-looking pattern by hand.

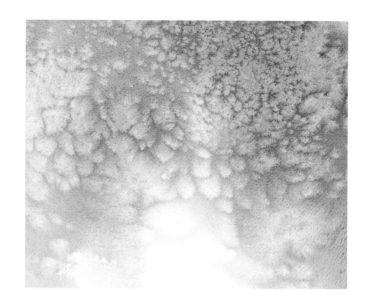

PAINTING A FALL OF SNOW

1 Begin by laying down a loose wet-in-wet wash of raw sienna and French ultramarine.

2 Wait for a minute or so, then sprinkle a few flakes of sea salt on to the damp surface.

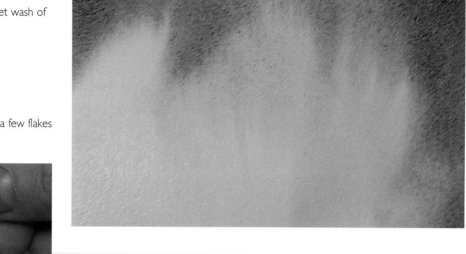

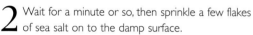

3 The sea salt soaks up the moisture from its immediate surrounding area. This is where timing will make the difference – add the salt too early, and the pattern it creates may be too large and unsightly. Leave it too late, and a lack of moisture may stop the effect from working at all.

5 Paint in the shapes of the cottage and walls with a mixture of burnt umber and raw sienna. Here, I painted it freehand, drawing with the brush, but you may feel happier lightly drawing it in first with a 2B pencil.

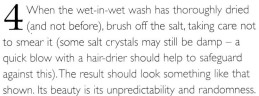

4 When the wet-in-wet wash has thoroughly dried (and not before), brush off the salt, taking care not to smear it (some salt crystals may still be damp – a quick blow with a hair-drier should help to safeguard against this). The result should look something like that shown. Its beauty is its unpredictability and randomness.

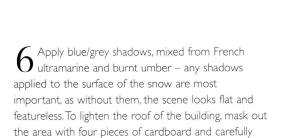

6 Apply blue/grey shadows, mixed from French ultramarine and burnt umber – any shadows applied to the surface of the snow are most important, as without them, the scene looks flat and featureless. To lighten the roof of the building, mask out the area with four pieces of cardboard and carefully scrub the paint away using a stencil brush.

7 Complete the painting by applying all the darkest tones, using a rich mix of burnt umber and French ultramarine. A simple scene such as this works better because of what you *can't* see than what you can see. Always try to inject a little mystery into your work by deliberately under-working it slightly. Here, the background hill has been graduated so it disappears into the snowfall, and the foreground wall is hinted at rather than clearly and accurately depicted.

USING MASKING FLUID

Rubber-based masking fluid can be used where you want to protect an area of paper either as a highlight, or to be painted over later. Its most common use is on subjects that require fine or delicate lines to appear light against a darker background, such as narrow branches or intricate under-growth. You quite simply apply the fluid like paint and wait for it to dry. Once it is dry, you can paint your background and the masked area will remain as untouched paper.

You should apply masking fluid with an old brush, a ruling pen (ideal for altering the size of the mark) or a rubber-ended 'colour shaper'. Extra protection can be gained by coating them in neat washing-up liquid (and wiping off the excess) before dipping them in the masking fluid. If you use a brush, clean it immediately afterwards in soapy water.

When the painting is completely dry, the masking fluid can be removed either by rubbing with the end of your thumb, or with a soft eraser.

A few notes of caution: it's not a good idea to leave masking fluid on too long; be aware that it just doesn't work on some soft-sized papers; don't apply it too thickly, or it'll take longer to dry and may strip the surface of the paper when you remove it; finally, don't be tempted to speed up the drying process with a hair-drier, or the fluid may melt into the paper.

WINTER SUNRISE OVER WHERNSIDE 17 × 26cm (7 × 10in)
To maintain the spidery fingers of the tree's bare branches as highlights meant protecting them first with masking fluid. The alternative of scratching out the branches afterwards was a possibility, but masking was the best option.

SNOW ISN'T ALWAYS WHITE

Like water (and, after all, that's all snow is), snow doesn't have any colour of its own. Although it's fine enough to show it as white in most circumstances (which is very much in keeping with our general notion of what the stuff looks like), in extreme situations snow can look far from white, and we should seize such opportunities when they present themselves to use snow as an excuse to disperse the available light and colours throughout a painting.

THE VALE OF EDALE FROM MAM TOR SUMMIT

17 x 26cm (7 x 10in)
As with the painting on the page opposite, this scene shows how snow appears to take its colour directly from the sky.

WINTER FEED 26 x 17cm (10 x 7in)

The snow in the middle distance has also taken on the colour of the background wash. The warm hue (mixed from cadmium yellow and burnt umber) on the fleeces of the sheep provided a subtle variation to an otherwise cold colour scheme, while the appearance of the tyre tracks in the foreground helped to give extra depth to the scene.

THE NOE STOOL, KINDER SCOUT

56 x 38cm (22 x 15in)
Here, the snow on the background hills has taken on the colour of the initial wet-in-wet wash (the orb of the sun was lifted out using a cardboard 'mask' and a stencil brush). As always, note the importance of blue-grey shadows on the foreground snow to suggest contours, and prevent the scene from appearing flat.

Project: Winter in Hartington

When sketching out a scene like this, I always begin as simply as possible by positioning its main elements. Although at first glance there appears to be a lot happening, it is very much a two-tone subject, therefore surprisingly easy to develop in pencil.

SKETCHING

1 There are several 'visual coincidences' present in the photograph that I was keen to rectify in the drawing, the most prominent being the alignment of the top of the right-hand walls. In the sketch, I deliberately stepped them so as to make them slightly more interesting. Then I went a stage further and made them appear less straight.

2 Next I shaded in the darker elements of the scene – the buildings, tyre tracks and wall.

3 As I defined the shapes, I also took the liberty of removing the lamp-post, since I didn't feel it would contribute in any way to the composition. Always feel free to take out, move or redesign objects to suit yourself.

PAINTING

 4 As always, I began by reproducing the basic layout on watercolour paper, using a light, weak burnt umber.

5 When I took the photograph, the sky was heavy and the whole scene was really quite grim. 'The sky's full of it' is a term I recall being used when I was younger; and as I pondered how best to develop this particular subject, I realized 'The sky's full of it' would be a good title for the scene, and I decided a warm wet-in-wet wash of alizarin crimson and French ultramarine would suit it admirably. Although the tyre tracks are barely visible in the source photograph, the decision to make them more prominent by turning them into puddles seemed a natural one to make. This gave me the opportunity to disperse the sky colour throughout the whole painting, and link the bottom and top halves together.

6 When the wet-in-wet wash was dry, I applied burnt umber with a touch of French ultramarine to all the walls and buildings, taking care to leave untouched highlights along the top edge of the walls and a few random highlights on the face of the nearest wall. I carefully worked around the spaces for the windows, and left a touch of burnt umber along the edges of the tracks.

7 Using French ultramarine with a tiny amount of burnt umber, I applied shadows to the walls and snow. When adding shadows to snow, think carefully about how they might look – every brushstroke counts, and even the smallest blob becomes an important part of the overall effect. Running a small amount along the edges of the highlights along the top of the walls transformed them from two-dimensional shapes into ones that were three-dimensional. As I had the blue/grey mix already in my pot, this seemed like a good time to add the background trees.

8 I completed the subject by painting in all the darkest tones. In the prominent right-hand wall, I didn't paint around all the stones, because I think the best stone walls are those that leave something to the imagination. Always try to say what you want to say in as few brushstrokes as possible; the painting will be stronger for it. Very often, those paintings in exhibitions with apparently the least amount of brushwork are the most striking.

FINAL THOUGHTS

How much to change a subject is a matter of personal choice. Although some might argue that altering things too much is not being entirely true to the subject, you should make no apologies for how you represent something in watercolour – any decisions you take must, ultimately, be beneficial to the composition. Painting, after all, should also be fun; although I may make my living through painting, the physical act of putting paint on paper still fascinates me as much as it did when I first started. It's a pleasurable process and a creative process: the challenge of exploring a scene and developing it into a more personal statement is something that interests me more than merely reproducing it.

One other thing: there is something a little bit scary about painting. It's so final. When the job is done and you review your work, there is always something there that makes you think, 'I could have made a better job of that bit,' or 'Perhaps I should have done it another way'. I think that drive towards perfection is what motivates many to carry on, even when the paint doesn't seem to want to do what you want it to do. However, try not to judge yourself too harshly – if you paint the perfect painting, you might just as well hang up your brushes, because there's nowhere left to go.

ADDING FIGURES

However wild and beautiful the landscape that inspires us to put paint to paper (and I'm assuming now that a love of the landscape is something that you and I have in common), we are these days never far from human activity – the rural landscape, after all, has been subjected to the reshaping and redesigning hand of man for centuries. Which brings me to the subject of people.

While I'm not overly fond of populating my paintings with too many people, there are times when the inclusion of one or more figures is going to be inevitable. A figure walking into, or across, a landscape can be used to remind the viewer that this is a location often visited by walkers or maintained by farmers. In some cases, a figure can be used as a compositional 'device'; for an example of this, see page 2 (and right), 'Sunrise over the Great Ridge'.

SINGLE FIGURES

When painting a figure in watercolour for landscapes, begin by reducing it to its simplest, most basic shape – think carrots! If you're a little unsure about painting figures, it's a good idea to paint them using a weak mix, so that, should they look embarrassingly un-human-like, you can lift them out with a piece of tissue.

Once you're happy with your carrot-like simple form, try dropping another colour into it while it's still damp. Figures are a great excuse for introducing bright, primary colours into a painting. Strange as it may seem, leaving a small gap between the head and the shoulders can also help the figure.

Finally, unless you actually want your figure to resemble a giant walking, talking vegetable, you might want to consider adding on a few extra limbs. Take care with this – you are unlikely to see all four limbs at the same time unless your figure is directing a jumbo jet at an airport. To give your figure a sense of realism and movement, consider adding only one arm or an extra leg to suggest catching it in mid-movement.

Unless your figure's name is Krusty the Clown, avoid showing its feet unless absolutely necessary.

MULTIPLE FIGURES

Figures provide narrative to a scene, so it is important for them to appear to interact with each other. Link them up – either by making them hold hands, or simply having them within close proximity to each other. Inclining their heads towards each other is an effective way of emphasizing that link.

IMPROVING FIGURE PAINTING

The best way to improve your figures is to observe people. How do they dress? What colours do they wear? What positions do they adopt when walking, standing, talking or running? If you're self-conscious about whipping out a sketchbook and drawing people *in situ*, position yourself in a discreet corner of a busy part of your local conurbation and take a few photographs to sketch and paint from later. The more you observe people in action and practise drawing them, the more natural-looking your results will be.

PROPS AND ACCESSORIES

Don't forget accessories: people wear hats and often carry bags, either in a hand or slung over their shoulder.

HUMAN PROPORTIONS

When drawing the human form, it's important to get the proportions correct. Of course, we all come in different sizes and shapes, but generally speaking, the body can be divided into seven equal segments. The head takes up only one segment, while the legs, from the bottom of the hips downwards, swallow up three segments.

FIGURES IN A SCENE

There are times when a painting requires the addition of human forms. For me, this is rare, since I invariably paint landscapes how I like to see them – which usually means no people. Occasionally, however, a painting needs life besides a few sheep or a flock of birds. A prime example is where figures provide a sense of scale, and another example would be a town scene.

PEAK DALE, CASTLETON
26 x 17cm (10 x 7in)
In this example, the small group of figures helps to explain the dimensions of their surroundings.

Project: Rhodes Old Town

The walled old town of Rhodes, on the Greek island of the same name, is a veritable rabbit warren of touristy craft markets and eateries, providing the artist with many potential subjects containing ancient old Mediterranean architecture and seriously sunburnt visitors.

SKETCHING

1 Having chosen the source photograph, I planned the scene out in sketch form, first, to familiarize myself with the figures, and to test out the overall balance of the composition. To do this, I began by drawing in the figures first (keeping them as simple as possible), then drew the trees and buildings around them.

PAINTING

2 For the painting, I began by lightly transposing the scene using a light, weak burnt umber and concentrating primarily on the figures themselves. I use a mix of raw sienna and alizarin crimson to represent flesh colour.

3 As soon as I was satisfied with my figures, I began painting in the background, using a mix of burnt umber and cadmium yellow to suggest warm stone.

4 When the first washes were dry, I applied blue/grey shadows throughout, mixed from French ultramarine and burnt umber.

5 Finally, I applied the darkest tones. The scene was kept deliberately loose to help suggest movement and activity, relying more on the use of shadows and sharp contrasts to give it strength than any serious attention to detail, whether human or architectural.

FINAL THOUGHTS

Speaking as one who sits for many hours in exhibitions longing for the telltale unclipping of a cheque book cover or the familiar flexing of a credit card, I must confess to a bit of a passion for people-watching. You try not to analyse or categorize people, but to deny yourself the fun of a little amateur anthropology is, I think, denying yourself one of the fundamental pleasures of acknowledging the existence of our fellow human beings.

For me, figures have to be placed into some sort of context. In this case, meandering visitors have simply added extra life and colour to an already beautiful and interesting corner of the world.

URBAN LANDSCAPES

Even if you are attracted to the natural landscape in preference to the man-made, it's worth taking a second look at urban conurbations once in a while, to see what's on offer in terms of raw material. Despite being a confirmed rural landscape painter, I'm always fascinated by the subtle juxtaposition of old and new when venturing into heavily populated areas, although I'm much happier moseying about small towns than battling with the manic pace of modern city living.

SKETCHING

Although brick isn't the only material you're going to come across when drawing buildings, it's the one most likely to cause problems.

The first sketch demonstrates a basic brick design, with each brick individually drawn out then carefully shaded in. This is OK if you want your wall to be of tidy, modern appearance.

If you want to 'roughen' the appearance a little, try the example on the left, where the bricks have been created using a plain shading pattern.

A third approach is this example, featuring bricks that are less uniform in tone, and with the addition of a few heavier lines to denote missing mortar. The result is less precise, suggesting age and decay.

OLDER BUILDINGS

Interesting corners can be found in any town or city, irrespective of size or age, if you only look for them. I chose just such a corner, tucked away in the Yorkshire town of Richmond, because it rather conveniently brings together several features.

1 I began by planning out the basic shapes of buildings in line form, and positioning the windows and doors. Note how all the horizontal lines slope downwards towards eye level, which is quite low in this composition.

2 I then began working on the wall detail. There are two distinctly different styles here: in the left-hand building, I picked out individual bricks, while in the right-hand building, I drew around the stones. Always look closely at how the building appears to you, and draw it accordingly – draw what you see, and don't be influenced by what you think you know about the building.

3 I completed the sketch by applying all the shadows and darkest tones. Note the hint of detail in the right-hand, foreground wall. Sketching, in its truest form, is all about gathering information and developing composition. It is the visual representation of a thought process. In the greatest tradition of sketching, you should neither overlook nor dwell on any one aspect of a potential painting; the addition of a small amount of stonework detail within what is quite a tonally dark area was sufficient to remind me later on of what that wall looked like, at least at a glance. In the final painting, below, I developed this wall quite considerably.

PAINTING BRICK AND STONE

There are two main methods of painting brickwork. One is to protect the mortar with masking fluid and apply the brick colour (here, burnt umber and cadmium red) over the whole surface area of the wall; however, the result of this, once the dried masking fluid has been removed, can be a little too tidy and new-looking.

The other method is to paint the bricks individually, without using masking fluid at all; the result is far more appealing and natural-looking. Even better is to paint the wall in two or three layers, varying the placing of the bricks and randomly softening and blending the paint with clean water to give a slightly indistinct appearance. Finally, if you want your wall to look weathered and slightly decrepit, pick out a few random bricks by overpainting them with a darker tone.

Stonework looks good if you vary how you paint it. Alternating between painting the actual stones, and painting gaps between the stones, helps to suggest a wall that is slightly uneven and could probably do with repair work.

In a subject packed with many different types of building material, I balanced it by not offering any real clues as to the nature of the left-hand, middle-distance wall, and only hinting at the cobbles and flagstones in the foreground. The concrete surface of the right-hand building also provided a welcome relief from the abundance of textures all around it.

Project: Marmaris Old Town

Marmaris is in Turkey. I visited it on a day's boat trip from the Greek island of Rhodes. The Old Town was an area I sought out to escape the awful commercialization and 'hard-sell' foisted upon day-trippers, and I found this little corner somewhere just off the harbour, near to Marmaris Castle.

SKETCHING

1 When sketching a group of buildings, I always begin by drawing their outer shapes first. Take you time over sketching, and keep your pencil lines light so they can be easily erased if you have to make minor corrections (or even major ones).

2 Once I was satisfied with the basic outline, I looked at where the light appeared to be coming from, and then applied an even shading accordingly; at the same time, I drew in the upper windows.

3 Very often, it's not until you sketch a subject like this that you really begin to understand it: I find that if I have to draw it, I tend to question beforehand what it is that I'm actually looking at. It's not crucial to understand every single nook and cranny in a subject, but it is important to work out how every part relates to the other. Is this wall in front of, or behind that one? Where does it actually join the main building? How does it join? These are all questions you should be asking yourself – not to become a better builder, but to try and make as much sense of your own sketch as you can.

4 What attracted me to the scene in the first place was its quirky, hidden-away quality. What I discovered only when I'd started sketching it was the pleasing way in which all the separate parts of the scene interlocked, as shown here by the overlay of red lines. This interlocking of shapes is important in painting – a composition will be weakened if its component parts do not link to each other in an aesthetically pleasing way, so it is worth viewing a potential subject from all angles to ensure getting its best side. Beware of coincidences – for instance, the vertical lines of two separate objects that coincide would be better adjusted by slightly moving one object, creating a dogleg, or by introducing a horizontal object to help break up the line.

5 I completed the sketch by adding the finer details, such as the aerials and the ivy. This kind of sketch is only intended to be a preparatory study, exploring the subject and noting details that are going to be important when I later develop it into a watercolour.

USING SKETCHBOOKS

I wrote 'green' on the ivy in step 5, just to remind me of its colour. A simple note like this is often sufficient. If you do feel you need to add more details, you will find that the more sketching you do, the more likely you are to develop a shorthand – a method of recording information that means something to you. Sketches are like a notebook in which you record things in a way peculiar to you – look after them!

I'm very protective of my sketchbooks, often valuing their content above my paintings, as they represent thoughts and ideas that are personal to me. If I lose a sketch in my studio (believe me – it's easily done), I can't rest until I've found it. On a positive note, that usually means the studio gets an overdue tidy-up in the process.

PAINTING

6 I began the painting by transposing the basic layout of the scene using a weak wash of burnt umber. I do this because I like my paintings to consist entirely of brushwork, preferring to keep all pencil-work for the sketches. That's not to say things can't be corrected. If I make a mistake, it can be dampened immediately with a clean brush and then lifted off with a tissue. Occasionally, I use pencil to plan a painting out, if it is of sufficient complexity or I'm really not sure of the subject. However, I find pencil lines a little obtrusive and slightly inhibiting, as there is a tendency to feel you have to keep strictly within the lines – but that said, artists have successfully combined the two media for many centuries.

7 I began by painting in the sky with a plain wash. Instead of my usual Winsor blue, I used tropical pthalo blue, which caught the Mediterranean sky quite well. I then painted all the greenery, using a mix of cadmium yellow and Winsor blue. Next, I applied a single shadow colour to the scene, using a light mix of French ultramarine, burnt umber and alizarin crimson for subtle warmth. This was applied in a blanket fashion, reproducing step 2 of the sketch, providing a starting point by breaking the whole design down into light and dark areas. With subjects like ivy, you should try to avoid creating patterns that are too even or repetitive; also take care not to create 'faces' that threaten to stare out at you every time you look at the painting (it's easily done, and you never spot them until it's too late).

8 Once the initial washes were completely dry, I began gradually building up the darker tones, a job that should always be handled carefully. Take your time and don't go in there like a bull at a gate – remember, it's easier to darken areas that are too light than to lighten areas that you've painted too dark. In addition, I incorporated plenty of graduation, both in the areas that required it, and in areas that I was still a little unsure of. If in doubt, graduate it by softening it with clean water – this can help to give you extra thinking time!

9 To complete the painting, I added the extreme dark tones and the finer details, such as the aerials. In the original source photograph and sketch, there was a white, curved structure visible in the gap between the middle and right-hand buildings. When it came to the painting, I felt happier leaving this out because I particularly liked the angular patch of blue sky there. Always remember that, in terms of painting design, the spaces between objects, the negative spaces, are themselves shapes that contribute to the whole composition.

FINAL THOUGHTS

This particular scene is something that could all too easily have been overlooked, had I not been of a sufficiently enquiring mind. When searching for potential subjects, I always try to give myself plenty of time to look at things from all available angles. In this case, giving in to the lure of following a few tiny alleyways not instantly visible from the main thoroughfare (and perhaps, occasionally, stepping into places I shouldn't really be), paid off.

In other words, be nosey! Don't always settle for the obvious – the 'big picture' is not always necessarily the best, most visually interesting or challenging composition. For every obvious viewpoint, there are usually two or three less obvious viewpoints just waiting to be discovered.

Outdoor sketching

Setting out on a sketching trip with little more than a sketchbook, pencil, waterproof clothing and provisions is without doubt my preferred method of working. It may not be to everyone's taste, but to anyone serious about landscape, I cannot recommend the activity highly enough if you want to really get to know your subject.

SKETCH *IN SITU*

 I chose this sketch specifically because it is one of the worst sketches I could put my hands on, and yet it sums up many of the fundamental aspects of sketching. It was one of the most unpredictable days, weather-wise, that I've been out in for many years, and at the time of scribbling this sketch, I was about to be heavily rained upon for the umpteenth time that morning. Consequently, this represents no more than about three minutes' work. Frantically, I drew the outer shape of the buildings and added the windows – the precise number and positioning of windows wasn't really that important (but it always seems important at the time). With the first drops of rain, my attempts to show the complex foreground of worn peat and gritstone were going to have to wait. I quickly drew the copse of trees and the line of the background hill; the shading of the sky and the meaningless scrawl in the top corner were little more than parting shots born out of my frustration. The rain had returned, and the sketchbook went back into my rucksack.

Poor as it is, however, the sketch contains all the necessary ingredients required for a painting. In those three frantic minutes, I'd collected a farmhouse, a copse of trees, a stone wall and the memory of a moment in time. Armed with my damp sketches and memories, I returned to my studio, dried myself and my equipment, and set to work.

STUDIO DRAWING

This was my first step towards developing the scene into a painting. The farm buildings, stone wall and trees are still there, but in a different, warm and relaxing environment I set about interpreting the subject in a more considered way.

After redrawing the farmhouse, I tried to make sense of the trees by tidying them up and introducing some dark, contrasting tones. My recollections of the day were sufficient to enable me to think through the foreground; I introduced the sheep as a form of compositional balance.

PAINTING

The painting reflects the fact that both sketches were done in October; my lousy sketching day was an isolated day of torrential rain among weeks of settled dry weather. Despite the rain, my feelings towards the subject were influenced by the gorgeous autumnal colours that had been in abundance around that time.

On another occasion, I might have wanted to re-create the bad weather of the day. My decision to paint it in an altogether different mood demonstrates something all landscape painters, whatever their ability, should consider. Generally speaking, all sketches start out as a line sketch that defines the rough shape of objects within the scene and how they relate to each other. This is an important point that is easily overlooked. It's not enough just to place objects at random within a composition – the objects must relate to each other, support each other and combine in a visually interesting and stimulating way.

When a sketch is translated into watercolour, similar priorities must apply. A pencil sketch made on site is an instantaneous response to the subject, and the natural desire to capture the essence of the scene, and to gather as much visual information as possible within the time allowed, is paramount.

A watercolour, on the other hand, is a separate beast entirely. Reality should never get in the way of a good composition – if, when deciding on how best to paint your sketch, you want to change things around, then go ahead. If it feels right, do it! Too often I've seen work spoiled because the simple desire to enjoy the act of painting and improvise on a scene has been overshadowed by unnecessary loyalty to the source material.

Of course we want to be true to the scene and want to capture what inspired us to think it might make a good painting in the first place, but a painting is a part of the artist, and the best painting is an honest painting. That doesn't mean you have to throw off the shackles of convention entirely, but individual expression has a place, too.

AUTUMN IN THE VALE OF EDALE Final painting
17 x 26cm (7 x 10in)

What to look out for

When planning a sketching trip, it's a good idea to have a loose agenda, whether it's going to be a 15-minute stroll or a 10-mile day-long hike. Set yourself targets, but don't over-stretch yourself and be sure to keep within your available time and ability.

When you're out there, keep an open mind. Be receptive to everything about you. You may know your route like the back of your hand, and you may well have earmarked several potential stopping-off points, but you should also be on the lookout for the unexpected, the things you simply cannot plan for.

OBSERVING THE DETAILS

Landscape is often thought of in expansive terms: the great panorama, the breathtaking vista. Of course these are primary objectives, but don't overlook the smaller things. That great landscape is made up of lots of little parts, each one a potential masterpiece. The very fabric of the land – here, where the ground has been worn away by the rain and wind, there, where an odd-shaped rock sits, partially obscured, amongst the long grass – is waiting to be sketched.

Look down at where you're walking as much as across at where you're walking to. These are things we take for granted. Stop and sketch anything and everything – even the most unlikely objects can turn out to be valuable. Keep your sketchbooks safe and well organized. Subjects can be imported into other paintings as well as forming compositions by themselves.

Be aware of the geology of the area in which you are walking – what type of stone or wood is used to construct local walls? Are shrubs, bushes or trees the norm? What materials are used in the construction of farm buildings? Is the roof made of tiles, metal sheet or slates? Every tiny piece of information that you can accumulate through looking and sketching will show up in some form or other at the easel. The more intimately you get to know your subject, the more informed your watercolours will be.

FROM SKETCH TO PAINTING,
Late September, Grindsbrook 17 x 26cm (7 x 10in)
This is another example of an outdoor sketch made in the rain. I always carry a medium-grade watercolour pencil with me since normal graphite pencils give up the ghost once paper gets wet. Being forced into working quickly is not altogether a bad thing – it helps to focus the mind. Concentrate on capturing only the basic, most important aspects of a scene – the second sketch, produced in the studio, was an opportunity to think through the subject at a more leisurely pace.

OBSERVATION

Successful sketching is all about observation. It would also be true to say that the more you do it, the better at it you will become. Remember, any sketch made out of doors is not necessarily the definitive version. It's all about getting to know your subject.

Making reference photographs

Carrying a camera with you is a must, particularly if you are in a place you're unlikely to return to for a while. A photograph or digital image can provide that extra piece of information you may find lacking from your sketch, but don't be tempted to slavishly reproduce it as a painting without first exploring it in sketch form. This is not a rule – it's a guideline. Much has been said against the use of photography in art, but I don't like to be too purist about such things. It's all information-gathering, and most artists use photography in some form during the production of their work.

Be on the lookout for light tones against dark tones. Make the most of them and, if necessary, exaggerate them; your composition will be all the stronger.

Note how objects relate to each other. The corner of this building is in line with the darkest part of the bridge archway, and the roof is on the same horizontal line as the top of the background building's chimney stack. Without this sort of observation, it's easy to overlook the obvious and create conflicting perspectives.

It's not necessary to sketch every stone in a wall – settle for a few visual hints to remind you of the construction.

Walk around and pick the best position from which to make your sketch. The tree provides an ideal foreground.

Studio sketches – exploring your subject

Always remember: nothing is set in stone. As a painter, you have the right to change things to suit the composition. Just be aware of the impact any changes might have. If you move the sun, your shadows are going to run off in a different direction. If you take the leaves off the trees, a little more of the scene is going to be visible to you. Foliage can be useful for hiding things, but removing it may mean that a degree of improvisation is required.

Contre jour

WENSLEYDALE SUNSET Finished painting
38 × 56cm (15 × 22in)

I was originally attracted to this scene by the way it was backlit. I'd been walking in the opposite direction, with the setting sun to my back. Sometimes, just turning and looking behind you can present you with a whole new prospect. My original outdoor sketch (above left) includes the note 'Contre jour' (meaning 'against the light') to remind me of the moment.

All the ingredients of the original on-site sketch were reproduced in the studio drawing (opposite, below left), with a few amendments and additions. I brought in the right-hand wall to act both as a balance, since I felt the composition was rather one-sided, and as a visual 'stopper', helping to enclose the main focus of the subject a little more. The introduction of puddles in the foreground was to help emphasize the track and to link the top and bottom halves of the scene together by bringing down colours from the sky.

FINSHED ARTWORK

The most noticeable thing about the final interpretation in watercolour is the change in season and the background tree jumping from one side of the track to the other. This was because, even in the studio sketch, it was too central. I also moved the sun itself. In its original position, both walls of the barn that were visible would have been in the shade. Moving the light source enabled me to bathe one wall in warm light.

Changing the format

In addition to developing the content of a scene, studio drawings can be used to test the viability of different formats. Just because you've drawn a scene in a standard sketchbook doesn't mean it can't be changed. When developing an idea, it's often worth considering how the subject might be adapted into a panoramic or portrait-shaped piece of work.

If you can't work out why a particularly troublesome finished painting lacks impact, it might just be that cropping the paper into a different shape will be the making of it. You can clearly see here how a studio drawing served as an aid to visualizing the scene differently.

TRANSITION FROM ORIGINAL SKETCH TO STUDIO SKETCH

Sometimes the decision to paint a scene in a particular format is made for you. It just calls to you, or you just can't help visualizing it in that way. On other occasions, it is nothing more than a creative way of experimenting with the material you have available. On this page, all the information in the original, on-site sketch has been included in the studio sketch. It has just been redistributed slightly to fit into a 'wide-screen' format. As well as feeling that the subject would lend itself quite readily to such a change in format, it also gave me the opportunity to rectify one of the major problems inherent within the first sketch – the background hill was far too central.

THUMBNAILS If you're unsure of what format to use, test the composition with simple pencil sketches. These don't have to be elaborate – simplified representative shapes placed in different ways should be sufficient. Such sketches are called 'thumbnail sketches'.

ADDLEBOROUGH FROM ASKRIGG Finished painting
17 × 56cm (7 × 22in)
The way the light fell upon this barn, creating a wonderful juxtaposition between warm and cool, attracted me to the scene. To maintain that visual contradiction throughout the rest of the painting I left a little patchy snow on the ground, the result being a more harmonious balance of tones and colours than if I'd gone the 'green grass and sheep' route as in the original sketch.

IMPROVING A PAINTING BY CROPPING

This series of images demonstrates how cropping a painting can change its appearance subtly, and hopefully for the better.

In the original version of this painting, the top of the left-hand wall and the road break the composition almost exactly into two equal halves horizontally. The two prominent trees are also rather uncomfortably central and equally balanced.

Cropping the painting shifts the focal balance, breaking the composition into more aesthetically pleasing thirds.
This is known as the rule of thirds.

BELOW EAGLE CRAG

13 × 28cm (5 × 11in)
Cropping can also be used to change the format from landscape to portrait. A cropped version of this Lake District scene can be seen opposite the Index at the back of the book.

Project: Rocks and sheep

Geological features make ideal subjects for watercolour. They punctuate the landscape, and can often be viewed from a multitude of directions – each one a different composition. Just when you think you know a subject, it goes and surprises you.

Never write off a location as a potential subject purely on the grounds of already having been there and done it – there is always something new to discover about any environment!

What attracted me most to this scene were its strong contrasts. These are ideal conditions for a scene depicting crags and rocks, because their most important feature is the material they consist of. Hard-edged, dark shadows give the impression of something you could cut yourself on.

SKETCHING

1 I began the sketch by defining the basic structural lines and shapes inherent within the composition. This means that I can ensure I get the scale and perspective right without making major corrections later on.

2 Because the tonal contrasts impressed me most, my next move was to shade in the darkest tones. It occurred to me that the position of the shadows strongly defined the actual position of the sun. Remember: a sketch is an ideal opportunity to explore your subject in depth, so never be afraid to improvise.

3 You may find that shading has a tendency to smudge things a little. Apart from this resulting in a dirty hand, don't worry too much about it. Here, I went back into the drawing, redefining the edges of shapes and accentuating the contrasts. I also drew in a few light lines to suggest undulations and shapes in the ground. These are important, as they help to draw the eye in towards the focal point, which was the top of the crag, somewhere near the two prominent standing stones. I added a few sheep at this point to bring a little life into what was otherwise a very static scene; they also helped to accentuate the focal point.

PAINTING

4 I began the painting by planning out the scene on watercolour paper, using a light, weak mix of burnt umber.

5 After contemplating the subject for some time, I came to the conclusion that, considering my positioning of the sun on the sketch, it would be nice to set it at sunrise, which would allow me to capitalize on the high contrasts as observed in the preparatory sketch. I began by laying down a warm wet-in-wet wash of cadmium yellow, cadmium red and French ultramarine. I kept the sun hazy and soft by painting around it while creating the wash; if I'd opted for a sharp, hard-edged sun, I would have lifted it out after the wash had dried.

6 I applied a pale green, mixed from French ultramarine and cadmium yellow, to the grass areas, and a weak transparent wash of French ultramarine to the distant line of hills.

7 When the washes were dry, I applied a warm, rich mix of French ultramarine, burnt umber and alizarin crimson to the dark-toned areas of the rocks. It was important, because the scene was backlit, to retain a highlight of untouched paper along the top edges of obviously the large stones, but also the smaller rocks lining the far edge of the escarpment. With stone, you shouldn't worry too much about the appearance of any backruns, since these contribute to the texture.

8 I used a medium-toned mix of burnt umber and cadmium yellow to break up the featureless surface of the greens. These subtle details are important to suggest contours of the land, both near and far. Take care, however, not to create patterns that are too repetitive or unnatural. I also added a small amount of detail to the background hills, using a light mix of French ultramarine.

9 I completed the sheep by applying a dark, rich mix of burnt umber and French ultramarine to the heads, then painted cadmium yellow and burnt umber on the bodies while the wash was still wet, so the two colours could bleed into one another.

10 Finally, I applied the darkest tones to create sharp, razor-like cracks on the rock face. A final smattering of blue/grey shadows completed the scene. Allowing your shadows to slightly overlap on to the lightest areas helps to give added shape to their edges. Be on the lookout for missed shadows. Consider where your light source is, and how it might impact upon objects within the scene. It would, for instance, be quite easy to forget to add the shadows cast by the sheep.

FINAL THOUGHTS

Although the basic ingredients of the original source photograph and pencil sketch are still present, this example clearly demonstrates how a scene can be transformed into something quite different just by lighting it in a more evocative way. Painting is a creative process in which you can, and should, draw upon a whole range of experiences, personal or otherwise. Who hasn't witnessed those first rays of sunlight in a morning and thought how lucky they were to be there at that very moment? There's every reason why that same macro-moment should be imported into a painting to evoke the same feeling.

I debated whether or not to apply a light, creamy glaze to the upper surface of the escarpment, in keeping with the mood of the scene and the low sun; however, in the end, I made a decision to leave it as white paper, fearing that a glaze might deaden the contrasts I'd been so keen to promote.

GALLERY

RIPOLL, PYRENEES

Pencil sketch and finished painting
17 x 26cm (7 x 10in)
I often like to compare the lighting of subjects in a painting to the lighting of a scene in a play or a film. What the sketch doesn't tell you is that only moments before stopping and drawing it, the heavens had opened and we'd been caught in an almighty downpour. My memory of the moment when the sun came out again is a strong one, and it helped to transform the scene in a creative and dramatic way. Memories should not be overlooked as a potential tool in your sketching armoury.

THE BRIDGE AT WATENDLATH

Pencil sketch and finished painting 28 × 38cm (11 × 15in) It was late on a midsummer's evening when I chanced upon this idyllic and perfectly placed packhorse bridge lit by the final dying rays of sunlight. Such moments are fleeting, and the sketch was actually made a few minutes later in gloomy half-light. The lighting effect was only re-established at the painting stage with the help of a vivid memory.

THE CHICKEN SHED

Pencil sketch and finished painting

28 x 38cm (11 x 15in)

Chickens don't usually feature much in my work; on this occasion, however, I was forced to make an exception. Although in reality the chicken shed was painted a vivid green, I chose to paint it in something more in keeping with the composition. Ultimately, of course, this is one of the pleasures of painting; the final decision is always yours to make.

WINTER REFLECTIONS (SHAW LANE, HAWES)

Pencil sketch and finished painting 38 × 56cm (15 × 22in)

Not so long ago all my winter scenes featured dark, cold, stormy skies. I've now grown out of my 'angry young man' phase, and prefer to show the juxtaposition of warm against cold by counter balancing snow with the colours of sunset or sunrise.

Several design changes can be seen in the transition from sketch to finished painting. The background barn has been moved to the opposite side of the paper to balance things up, preventing everything from sloping off to the right. The sheep, too, are a compositional 'ploy', introduced to help give added interest to the focal point, and provide the eye with a visual 'stepping stone'. This is not an absolute rule, but grouping sheep or cattle in odd numbers is often a good idea – likewise, sheep placed close to the edge of the paper should be looking inwards, towards the centre, not out, beyond the borders of the painting.

WHITFIELD GILL FORCE, ASKRIGG

Pencil sketch and finished painting 28 × 38cm (11 × 15in) Although the fall itself provides the centrepiece of the composition, I wanted to show how closed in its location is, but still bring sufficient light into it. My solution was to exaggerate what little light there was. The few reference photographs I took at the time were far too dark to be of any substantial use, proving the priceless value of the humble pencil sketch.

Index

Acknowledgements

I would like to thank Mic Cady, Lewis Birchon, Sue Cleave and Ian Kearey, and everyone else at David & Charles who has been involved in the production of this book for making it all possible.

    I would like to thank all those dedicated students of art with whom I've come into contact over almost 20 years of demonstrating and teaching who have continued to ask the right questions and have forced me to constantly look deeper and deeper at my own work for the answers.

    Finally, I would like to thank Annette for reminding me that there is a world away from the easel.

Opposite:
BELOW EAGLE CRAG (detail)
28 × 38cm (11 × 15in)

Endpaper:
CAIRN ON HAYSTACKS
28 × 38cm (11 × 15in)

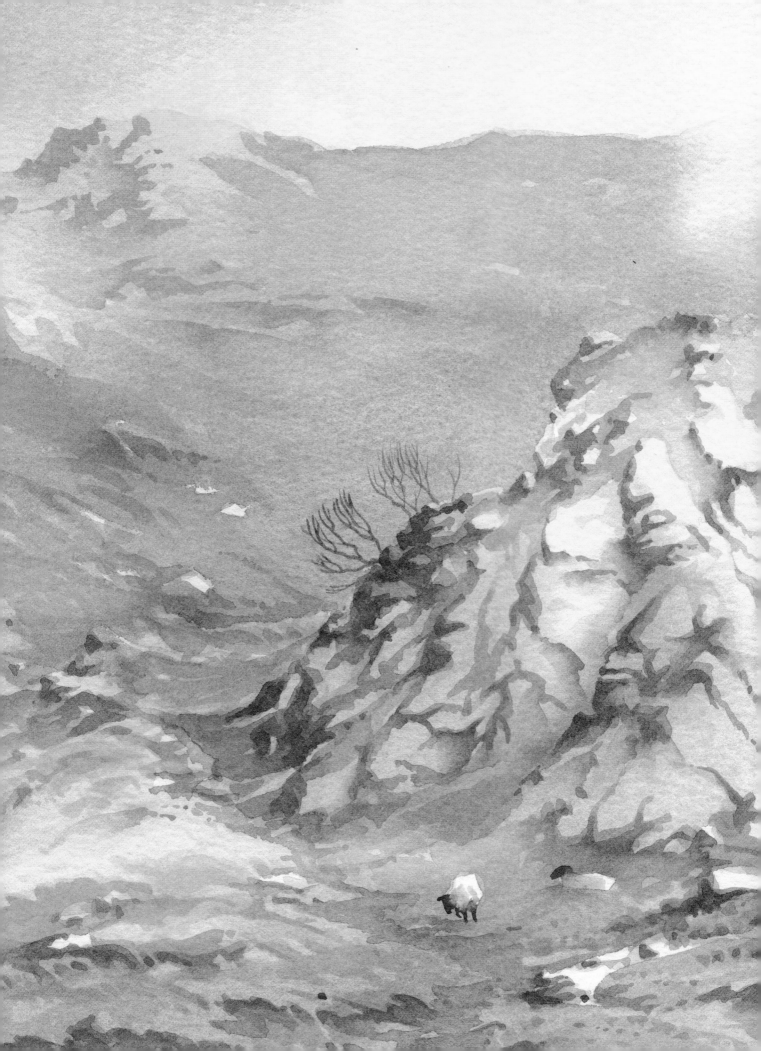